HOW TO

WRITE A NOVEL BEFORE YOU TURN 13

13 Steps for Kids to turn Creative Writing into a Book

BY OLLIE OOD

CHARACTER ILLUSTRATIONS BY ALEJANDRO MIRANDA

ISBN: Print 978-1-7780125-0-1 | eBook 978-1-7780125-1-8

CalamariTales.com

TABLE OF CONTENTS

13 STEPS WORKSHEETS

PAGES 165 TO 207

Download our guide on

HOW TO WRITE GREAT DIALOGUE

BookHip.com/JLJAFNK

INTRODUCTION

The idea of writing a novel can sound big and impressive. It's fun to tell your friends, "I'm writing a novel!"

But it can quickly become overwhelming and you start to think, "Wow. How do I write a story this big?!"

Maybe you've tried to write a novel before, only to have it fizzle out after a few chapters. Or, maybe you've never tried to write one but you think it would be fun.

Starting to write a novel is like cleaning your room—it sounds easy until you begin. Then you find the old bowl of mac n' cheese under the bed, and enough socks lying around to clothe an octopus family reunion. Each layer you dig into seems to breed more mess underneath. Pretty soon, you fall in a heap on the floor imagining you will be 85 and still cleaning up this mess. The whole thing feels impossible!

Writing a novel can feel like that. But it doesn't have to. While writing a novel is a big project, just like cleaning a messy room, it's not impossible. The key to big projects is breaking them into smaller chunks so that you don't fall into despair. You pick up one book, one section of Legos, a couple of dirty dishes.

You keep picking up one thing at a time, you don't stop; and eventually there is nothing left to do. The cool thing is, it often takes less time than you think.

Big projects are completed by small choices.

This is the same with writing a novel. This book will show you, step by step, how to take your story ideas and help them grow into a tale you can turn into a novel. As you read along, you'll get a road map for the sometimes wild, rough, and always adventurous journey of writing your own book. You don't have to set off whacking your way into the jungle blindfolded! Others have made this journey before you, I've done it, and even kids your age have done it. You can follow the paths and trails left by other writers, learn from their mistakes, and listen to their advice on how to avoid pitfalls and dead ends.

So, what do you say? Are you ready to set off on the adventure of writing your own book?

Let's go!

Ollie Ood

The 13 steps are all you need to create your novel. Follow each one and you'll end up with a story you can be proud to share!

13 STEPS

TO WRITE YOUR NOVEL

Listen to your creative ideas

Listen to your imagination and find your story idea.

Build your foundation

Take your idea and transform it into a one-page story.

Create character profiles

Get to know the characters who will star in your story.

Choose your point of view (POV)

Choose who is telling the story.

Decide on locations and settings

Decide where and when your story will take place.

Plan your story's plot

Plan out all the events in your novel.

Divide your plot into chapters

Create the building blocks for a full novel.

Set up some action

Add the elements that make a lively and dynamic story.

Write great dialogue

Discover how to make your characters speak.

Build to the climax

Mix together all the tension and action you've been creating.

Resolve your story

Tie up all the loose ends.

Revise and edit

Take a good story and make it great

Publish your book

Turn your manuscript into a real book.

MY NOVEL

STEP 1

LISTEN TO YOUR CREATIVE IDEAS

"I want to write a story, but I don't know what to write!"

Have you ever felt like this? Before you can write a novel, you need a story idea.

Sometimes we have a glimmer of an idea, some little phrase, or an image that comes to us when we're daydreaming. Perhaps you're walking in your yard, and you wonder what it would be like to have grass up to your waist. Then you wonder what it would be like to be a tiny person. Suddenly, your imagination shifts into high gear and you see your back yard, and your approaching cat, in a whole new light!

This is how ideas are born. Stories are our minds' way of trying to make sense of and order things we see (or imagine) into a logical chain of cause and effect—you know, since this happened, this other thing happened. We like there to be reasons behind why people do things. If we don't see the reason, we often make them up.

Observe, Daydream, and Brainstorm

If you don't have an idea yet, take some time to brainstorm. Go lie out in the grass. Ride your bike. Take a sheet of paper and write everything that comes into your mind for three minutes straight. Pay attention to everything around you—anything can be a story.

Storytellers are first and foremost "observers." They notice things. Don't rush through your day, wolfing down that hamburger, running here and there. The key is to slow down, see the exciting things around you, and let your imagination know you are ready to listen. Your imagination is with you all the time, but sometimes we do a pretty good job of squashing it. Stop doing that! Let your mind wander and see where it takes you.

Idea Mash Up

When you have an idea, you can try to narrow it down. Let's say you want to write a story about pigs acting like people. So, you take that a little further and ask, how exactly would the pigs act like people? What would that look like? Where would they go? See if you can turn your idea into a question like, "What if pigs taught at my school?"

You've probably already made up thousands of stories in your life!

All you have to do is ask, "What if..." and you're on your way to a great story idea!

The weirder and stranger the two elements of your *what if*, the better! You might be thinking, "But I can't think of anything out of the ordinary." The great thing is, two ordinary things mashed together can make something unusual and fun. And that little bit of unusualness in your idea will make it compelling to readers.

If we wanted to create a template for a type of story idea, we could say:

What if one ordinary thing or person (like a pig) found itself in a situation that was unusual for them (like a school)?

Not all stories fit into this pattern, but if you are stuck, taking something usual and mashing it with some other unusual quality, or putting a person in a unique place or circumstance, might get you started.

Narrow Down Your Ideas

Once you have a story idea or many ideas, it's time to see which one will be best for a novel.

First of all, do you like your idea? Does it excite you? Do you think there is enough to your idea that you could write about it for a while? Does it seem to have lots of possibilities of where the story could go? These are qualities you want in a novel idea.

Some ideas make for a good joke, or a short story, or a little comic strip. But a novel idea has to be a *different* idea. It has to be big enough to hold a whole world inside it, with lots of possibilities. What if an orphan boy found out he was a wizard? And what if he discovered an entire wizarding world that he never knew of before? See what I mean? There's a reason the idea for *Harry Potter* could last through seven books!

If you have an idea and instantly your brain is taking off in a million different directions, exploring various possibilities, you might have found the right concept.

Turn your Idea into a Question

You may have noticed all the ideas I listed are written as a question. What if…, what happens when…, when this happens, who will…. If your idea is not a question yet, go ahead and try to turn it into one. Framing it as a question will help you start to think about it in terms of what happens in your story. This is important because to change an idea into a story, events and actions need to happen. So, your brainchild changes from rabbits who live in a town to *What happens when* rabbits who live in a town suddenly have to move?

Do you see how framing your story as a question instantly brings up other questions? Now we want to ask, why do they have to move? So, we answer with, because a fox has moved into the neighborhood. Then we can ask, where will the rabbits go? If we want to intensify things, we can make it so the rabbits know the fox is coming, but he isn't there yet. As they make plans to move, they realize problems that make it hard to move quickly. Do they have old rabbits who can't move? Have they already moved enough and are sick of it?

Now the question changes to what happens when rabbits who live in a town suddenly have to move, but they can't, or don't want to? That small change gives us the makings of a great story where exciting events unfold, and not everyone wants the same thing. This potential clash between the rabbits and the fox is the conflict that will make this story interesting!

As you write out your questions, don't be afraid to change your initial idea as the questions lead you to explore your story.

Look for ways to make things harder on your characters, even if you don't know them very well yet. This will make your story feel satisfying to your readers. In other words, they'll like it! I could've made the rabbits find an easy path to a new, better home. The end. That would be a story, but it wouldn't be a *satisfying* story.

So, what makes a satisfying story? Struggles, conflict, overcoming. We love to read about characters who have to fight for what they want or even who have to figure out a problem. Problems and conundrums make for good stories that keep us interested. Because now, as readers, we feel invested in the story. We want to see how the characters will solve their problems and what happens in the end.

Now that you have an idea you are excited about, it's time to think a bit about how to build your story. This is especially important for a long story, such as a novel. Just like the house you live in has a structure or frame that everything is built upon, stories also have a structure. Most stories, in their simplest form, have a three-part structure. You are already used to narratives with this pattern—Beginning, Middle, and End.

In the next chapter, we'll show you how to build the foundation to base your novel on.

STEP 2

BUILD YOUR FOUNDATION

Now it's time for your newborn idea to become a real story. Before you can turn your story into a novel, you need to figure out what will happen in it and who it will happen to. Let's try this exercise:

Take your idea and turn it into a one-page story. This should be very brief and just tell the facts of what happens, who your characters are, and the problem they are trying to solve. Use the brainstorming we started in the last chapter with the "What happens when..." questions.

If a novel is a house, this one-page story will be your foundation—what you build the rest of your house on. This one-page story will guide you as you build the rest of your book.

After you've written it, look it over. Have you given your characters something they want or need? Have you created something or someone standing in their way from getting it? What can you throw into your character's way to make it harder to reach their goal?

Three Sample Stories

Throughout this book, I will be developing three story ideas to show you how to build a story, and these tales will be used as examples as we learn the different parts of writing a novel.

The first idea is about an ordinary girl who finds herself in an unusual circumstance. I'm calling it *Junie and Roger Get Zapped*. What happens when a girl, Junie, and her small dog, Roger, end up in a strange electrical accident and find they can now talk to each other telepathically (through their minds)?

The second idea is called *Fairies in the Baseboards*. What happens when two newbie/apprentice tooth fairies get separated from their class and left behind in a human house while on a field trip? What adventures will they get into as they wait for their teacher to rescue them and as they try to hide from the curious kids who live there?

The third and last idea is called *The Bully Club*. What happens when a boy who's constantly been bullied starts a club for kids like him who've had enough? Will they be able to move past the bullying and see their bullies as people, or will they be caught up in revenge and inadvertently become bullies themselves?

Use these to get an idea of how yours should look and how long it should be.

Fairies in the Baseboards

Gabby and her friend Tito sit in class and learn about the dangers of encountering Humans. Gabby tries to pay attention even though she has doubts about the information. They are students in the Tooth Fairy School. The next day, on a field trip to a Human house with their Tooth Fairy School, Gabby can hardly wait to look around, but Tito is nervous. She decides to hide when it is time to leave, and only Tito notices she is missing and goes to look for her. When the class leaves, Gabby and Tito get left behind!

Due to the High holiday of Summer Solstice the next day, all traveling is prohibited after sundown the night before. No one will be coming for them until the following sundown—a whole night and day in the Human world alone!

Gabby didn't plan on this but she realizes this is a fantastic opportunity. She tries to convince Tito to calm down.

The fairies are clumsy and cause some accidents, so the children of the house, and especially the family's cat, soon suspect something unusual is going on. After several near misses, and one terrifying encounter with the cat, Gabby reveals herself to the children for help. The kids take the fairies to hide in their bedroom upstairs.

The kids are delighted and set the fairies up in their dollhouse. At first, it is amazing. Gabby feels like a queen in such a big house! But soon, Gabby becomes disappointed when the kids seem to think the fairies are toys to be played with (and fought over). She begins to think maybe she misjudged the kindness of Humans when one of them hurts Tito's arm. The children notice her sadness and realize the fairies aren't toys.

They stay up, making a tent with their sheets, and Gabby and Tito light it up by making their wings glow. The fairies and their new Human friends share stories and learn about each other's worlds. Then they all fall asleep.

Gabby is awakened, sleeping on the girl's bed, to a rescue team (kind of like a fairy SWAT team). She wakes up Tito. But before they can leave, the cat nearly pounces on them. The girls wake up and help the fairies escape.

Gabby and Tito are taken back to their world, and everyone wants to know how they survived interacting with the Humans (who have such big teeth). Gabby's friends crowd around her. Did they try to eat her? How did she manage to be so brave? Tito loves to tell all the stories, but Gabby just wants to go home. Back at her home, she starts in on her homework. She opens the book, and the chapter is "Avoiding being eaten by Humans." She shuts the book and instead makes a tent with her sheet, lights it up inside, and opens her notebook. She writes, "*Chapter One: The Humans We Never Knew*."

DO YOU LIKE THIS STORY?

YOU CAN HAVE IT!

USE IT ANY WAY YOU WANT!

JUNIE AND ROGER GET ZAPPED

Junie is a shy kid who doesn't have many friends and often sits in her closet and talks to her best friend Roger, her small white dog. Junie and Roger go on a walk every day, rain or shine. One day, on a drizzly walk, Junie sees a poster for a missing dog from a neighbor (a new family that just moved in). Dark clouds roll in, and Junie tries to head home, but Roger pulls her, chasing a squirrel. The squirrel runs up a giant oak tree at the edge of a park full of trees.

As Roger barks, climbing at the tree, lightning strikes the oak and sends electricity down the tree, into Roger, up the leash, and into Junie. The two of them are knocked back onto the grass. As Junie comes to, she realizes she and Roger can now hear and talk to each other through their minds!

They meet a girl named Macy. The lost dog on the posters is hers. Junie wants to help Macy and figure out the mystery. She thinks it might be boys who always tease Roger, but Roger says it was the squirrels. Junie confronts the boys but then realizes she was wrong. Roger claims all squirrels try to get dogs to run away. After several other failed leads, Junie and Roger fight, and Junie ends up sitting alone in her closet. Then she hears a voice and realizes it is a squirrel—the squirrel from the lightning tree! She deciphers his strange message and admits he may have had something to do with the dog's disappearance. After a showdown in the woods, they catch the squirrel in a shoebox and force him to talk. He admits they got the dog to run all around in the dark woods and get lost.

They let him go, and Roger says he knows where the dog is! Dog legend tells of a sausage lady, four blocks over, who puts out fresh food for all the animals every day. They hurry there and find the missing dog and take him back to Macy.

Macy and Junie decide to hang out the next day and let their dogs play. Junie and Roger walk home, content they could solve the mystery.

OR, DO YOU LIKE THIS STORY?

YOU CAN BUILD YOUR STORY OFF THIS FOUNDATION OR CHANGE ANY DETAILS YOU LIKE

THE BULLY CLUB

Three boys, Oliver, Jay, and Brayden, who are all teased, decide to join forces and become a club. Word gets around, and the club grows. Suddenly, they are a big group outnumbering the bullies. They call themselves the Bully Club.

Oliver is the leader. He is skinny and small for his age. He's been picked on his whole life. The kids start doing things to the bullies. Minor pranks at first, but then it grows to meaner and meaner things. Oliver especially seems to delight in it and leads the other kids to do more and more. Sometimes Oliver can even be mean to Jay, who is chubby and terrible at sports. Jay doesn't like it but doesn't stand up for himself. Brayden, who was popular at his old school but bullied now as a new kid, gets to know two brothers who sometimes hang out with the bullies. He starts to see them as friends. He learns they like driving ATVs, which he likes to do as well. He secretly starts hanging out with them but feels torn at school to reveal his new friendship to the rest of the Bully Club.

Oliver finds out about Brayden's friendships and kicks him out of the club. Jay quits too. Oliver enjoys the power of being on top, but when he does something exceptionally mean, he sees the effect on his victim's face. It's the same look Oliver has had many times. He doesn't like who he has become at all.

On the last day of school, Oliver goes up to the bullies at lunch and asks if he can sit with them. One boy says, "no way," and storms off. The boy who is left says sorry for all the things he did to Oliver in the past. Oliver also apologizes. Then they talk and find out they have a lot in common. While they probably won't be friends, Oliver comes away feeling changed. A couple of young club members challenge Oliver over his actions, but Oliver rips off his bully club button and throws it away. "You do what you want," he says, "but I'm tired of clubs."

Jay and Brayden call Oliver over, and the three of them decide to hang out.

HOW ABOUT THIS ONE?

YOU CAN USE THIS ONE TOO!

USE IT AS IS, OR CHANGE
ANY OR ALL THE DETAILS!

WHAT TO BUILD ON YOUR FOUNDATION

This one-page story is the foundation of your novel. If your novel were a house, it would need a foundation, but it would also need certain rooms to be considered a good house. Just like you have to have a kitchen, a bathroom, and a bedroom, your novel needs certain things too.

These are the... bricks that... will make a strong story

CHARACTERS
SETTING
PLOT
CONFLICT
RESOLUTION

Let's explore a few of the main qualities that make a novel successful.

Characters

Most of us already know what characters are. If you read the same book as your friends, you might chat about your favorite characters. Like we said earlier, "characters are the people (or animals, or aliens) who are living and acting out your story." They are the citizens of your story town, and all the action and plot events of the novel revolve around them. The main character is the star of the book. In the tooth fairy story, we have two main characters—Gabby and Tito. In your novel, this will be the character who is center stage in your narrative. You will have secondary characters too, these might be friends, teachers, enemies, etc., but their stories revolve around the main character. We'll talk more about characters in the next chapter, but for now, just remember characters are essential, especially creating a likable main character that your readers can identify with and follow along on their journey.

Setting

The setting of a story is the place or world where everything happens. If the story isn't set in contemporary times (that means today and not in the past), the setting will also include *when in time* the story takes place, such as Ancient Rome or the prehistoric 1980's or 90's when your parents were kids.

If your setting isn't crucial to your story, it could occur almost anywhere, but you still need to think about setting for individual chapters and scenes. Everything that happens takes place somewhere concrete and authentic to your story. We don't need pages and pages of description, that would be a snooze-fest, but we do need to know where events are happening and maybe the time of day if it's relevant. Don't let your characters float in front of a blank background—fill it in a little.

Plot

You can think of the plot as the events that happen in the story. It isn't just the story idea that tooth fairies are left behind in a house, but the actual things that happen in the story. The events unfold and, ideally, build upon each other. As you plan out your plot, a helpful question is, "What happens next?" or "And then what happens?" For example, the tooth fairies are left behind, and then what happens? Maybe they have to figure out a way to send a message to their teacher but to do that, they have to make it to the bathroom to use toothpaste and floss to create a "tooth fairy phone." But going to the bathroom can be complicated because a big fat cat is sleeping right in front of the door. See what I mean?

Plot is made up of your characters striving to reach their goals, in this case, to send a message and ultimately be saved, but the actions and events of others get in their way. I've heard it said that your characters don't know it isn't the end of the story.

In other words, they are trying and hoping to succeed and reach their goal with every choice they make. But we know that good and satisfying stories have problems that aren't easily solved. So, our characters try, fail, and try again. All the things they do, and the things that happen to them, make up the plot.

Conflict

It's hard to imagine a story without conflict. The late British author John Le Carré said it best, "'The cat sat on the mat' is not a story. 'The cat sat on the dog's mat' *is* a story." What's the difference between these two sentences? Conflict!

Conflict keeps a story interesting and intriguing. Who cares if a cat sat on a mat! But if a fight is about to break out because the cat took the dog's mat, that's interesting. If the dog is the main character and that darn cat keeps one-upping him all the time, we feel sympathy for the dog and look forward to how he finally puts that cat in her place once and for all. If, however, the cat is the main character, and the dog is constantly chasing her, maybe we will relish her decision to stand up for herself and take that bed for her nap.

Every chapter and scene of your novel should have conflict built into it. This isn't as hard as it sounds. As long as you have characters who want different things, or obstacles keeping them from easily getting what they want, you'll have conflict.

Resolution

While we do love conflict, we don't love conflict that goes on and on forever. Have you ever watched a movie where you think the bad guy is finally defeated, only to have them pop up again and again? Movies love to do this. But sometimes, a movie does it too much. The bad guy comes back, is defeated, comes back again, is defeated a second time, but then keeps coming. This is about the time people start wriggling in their seats. Why? Because ultimately, what we want is resolution.

What does resolution mean? It means the events and problems that the story has created are *resolved*. The problem is solved, the quest is complete, and we can finally go to the bathroom after drinking that large soda. Conflict makes the story interesting, but resolution makes the ending satisfying. It makes us feel like all is right with the world again.

Does a novel have to have resolution? No, it doesn't. But if you want people to like your story and feel like it is a *complete* story, I suggest you resolve the problems you create.

BUT MAKE SURE YOU SOLVE THE CONFLICT BEFORE YOU END THE BOOK!

All of these things, Characters, Plot, Setting, Conflict, and Resolution, will begin to take shape as you build upon your one-page story foundation and create the framework for your novel.

Next up, we will dive into one of the most critical parts of your whole story—the characters! After all, this is *their* story. You may think it's your story, but they are here to tell you otherwise.

STEP 3

CREATE CHARACTER PROFILES

So, what are characters? They are the people or beings who inhabit your story.

In the story of your life, you are a character. You are actually the main character. This is the person who the story is really about. Your friend, Hayden, might appear in your narrative, your mom and dad might show up, even your dog could make an appearance, but they are secondary characters. If you are the main character, everything in the story is ultimately about you (what you do, what you feel, how you grow). This is your story!

All kinds of characters show up in stories. Let's look at some examples of character types and figure out which characters from *The Wizard of Oz* they might be:

Protagonist

This is almost always the main character, and they are often good. In our case, this is Dorothy, of course.

Antagonist

This is the villain. You can have more than one, but usually, you have one main one. Obviously, it is the Wicked Witch of the West.

Supporting Characters

Usually friends of the Protagonist. Here we have the Scarecrow, the Tin Woodsman, and the Cowardly Lion.

Sidekick

Toto!

Love Interest

Um, not in this story.

Confidant or Mentor

This is a wise, usually older person the Protagonist can go to for help and wisdom. Here we have the Wizard and Glinda.

Foil

This is a character that is usually the opposite of the Protagonist in some way. In this case, Auntie Em, with her Midwestern practicality and no-nonsense, is the opposite of passionate Dorothy who dreams of places "over the rainbow."

See how you can work some of these character types into your story, or which category some of your existing characters fall into.

The next step is to develop the characters for your novel. Creating characters is another way of saying, "getting to know your characters," or making them feel as real as possible to you and your readers. Understanding your characters and why they act the way they do will help you write well-rounded characters that jump off the page.

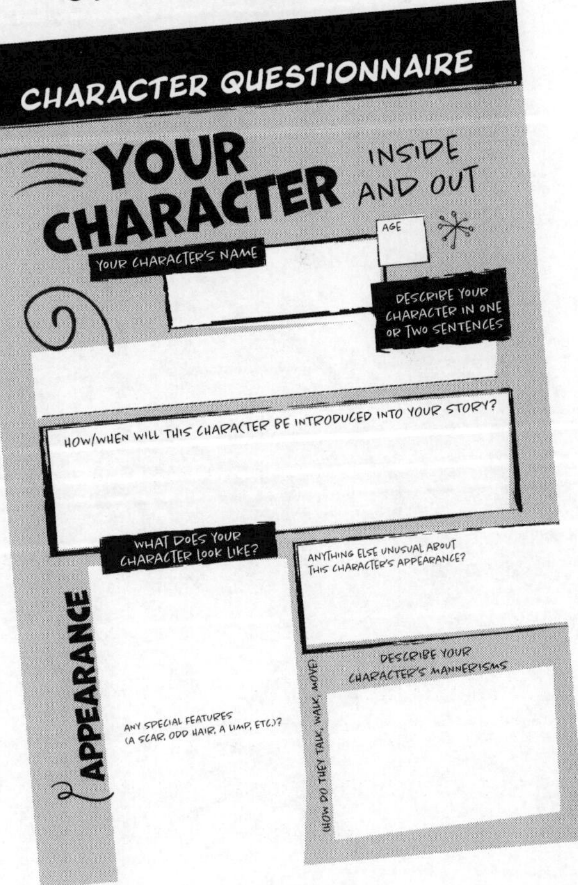

One trick to get to know your characters is to create a profile for them. There's a Character Questionnaire located at the back of the book on page 170 that will help you get to know your characters.

WHAT MAKES AN EXCELLENT MAIN CHARACTER?

It is very likely you already have an idea who your main character will be. Remember, the main character is the person who the story is about. Some characters show up in a story, like the Scarecrow, but the story isn't really about what the Scarecrow wants and does. The character central to the whole story is Dorothy. She is the main character.

Not all characters have what it takes to be an excellent main character. Your main character, obviously, will be the character you spend the most time with. They are also the character who has to win over your readers if you hope for your book to succeed. So, what makes a great main character? There are three main qualities: someone active, someone interesting, and someone likable.

Active

An active character makes choices in the story. They make things happen. They go after what they want. Characters who don't take charge of the story and let it push them from thing to thing are passive. Passive characters are okay for secondary characters but not for the star of the show. And your main character is the star!

Interesting

An interesting character has something about them that draws us in. Maybe they are "the boy who lived," or perhaps they have some other remarkable quality, like a spunky personality, and we can't wait to see what they will do next. Maybe they are very brave or so passionate about doing the right thing that we are intrigued by the choices they make. Or, maybe they're so goofy and always getting into trouble that it's fun to go along for the ride. Whatever the case, we know a story with this character won't be dull.

Likable

A likable character is, above all, someone we can connect with. As we read stories, we actually align ourselves to the main character. In other words, we experience the story as if it were happening to us! But we can't fall into the story world and have the same adventures if we don't like the main character. We need to connect to their heart. Main characters have to let us in to see their weaknesses, fears, and struggles. We connect with Dorothy because most of us have felt we don't belong at one time or another. We also connect with her later on in her quest to go home because we know what it's like to be lonely and to long to go where we are loved best of all.

Let's look at the main character from Fairies in the Baseboards. I filled out a few character questions for the main character, Gabby.

YOUR CHARACTER INSIDE AND OUT

YOUR CHARACTER'S NAME

Gabby

AGE

12

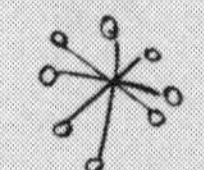

DESCRIBE YOUR CHARACTER IN ONE OR TWO SENTENCES

Gabby is a young, brave fairy with an adventurous spirit. She is in Tooth Fairy School as a first-year student.

HOW/WHEN WILL THIS CHARACTER BE INTRODUCED INTO YOUR STORY?

In the opening scene, sitting in class learning about how dangerous humans are.

APPEARANCE

WHAT DOES YOUR CHARACTER LOOK LIKE?

Gabby has dark wavy hair, brown eyes, and olive skin. She is three inches tall and the tallest in her class. She wears a tan muslin dress that hangs straight and has holes for her wings, like most fairy girls her age. She has a leather belt and leather shoes.

ANY SPECIAL FEATURES (A SCAR, ODD HAIR, A LIMP, ETC.)?

She has sheer wings that have beautiful swirling patterns that light up green when she chooses to turn them on. All the fairies have unique wing patterns.

ANYTHING ELSE UNUSUAL ABOUT THIS CHARACTER'S APPEARANCE?

No

DESCRIBE YOUR CHARACTER'S MANNERISMS (HOW DO THEY TALK, WALK, MOVE)

Gabby is always looking around and taking in all she can. She is easily bored and always looking for something to do.

CHARACTER QUESTIONNAIRE

PERSONALITY

DESCRIBE YOUR CHARACTER'S PERSONALITY (LOUD, CHEERFUL, SHY, GRUMPY, ETC.)

Gabby doesn't tell everyone her thoughts. She is private about her longings to explore the Human world. She secretly doesn't believe humans are as bad or dangerous as the books say. She is resourceful and strategic. She wants to research and write her own books someday.

DO THEY HAVE ANY UNUSUAL THINGS ABOUT THE WAY THEY ACT?

Gabby is skeptical about what she's been taught, which is very unlike other fairies in her village.

DO THEY LIKE TO BE WITH OTHERS, OR DO THEY PREFER TO BE ALONE?

Alone

CHARACTER'S PAST

DID THEY HAVE A GOOD UPBRINGING OR NOT?

Gabby has a very happy home life, even though her mother is very strict.

DID ANYTHING BAD HAPPEN TO YOUR CHARACTER THAT FORMED WHO THEY ARE TODAY?

Gabby's grandmother once told her a story about her experience with Humans and ever since then Gabby has wanted to have a similar experience.

WHERE ARE THEY FROM?

A Fairy village

WHO IS YOUR CHARACTER CLOSEST TO? (THIS CAN BE WITHIN THE STORY OR INCLUDE OTHERS NOT IN THE STORY AS WELL)

Her grandmother but Tito is becoming a good friend.

As I filled this in, I realized some changes I wanted to make to my one-page story, so I went back and added new details. That is perfectly fine! Your one-page story can change (and probably will) as you learn more about your characters.

So how exactly do you work details about your character into your writing? Here is how I first introduce Gabby in this story. It begins with Gabby and Tito sitting at the back of the class:

I waited until Professor Fauna turned back to her map of a typical Human house. She continued to drone on about possible escape routes should the vicious Humans awaken while on a tooth run. Give me a break! Tito was busy scribbling notes. I leaned over my book and let my dark wavy hair cover it. No wonder Mother would never let me explore when every book was written to make the Humans look like fairy-eating monsters. Professor Fauna whipped around and called my name. "Gabby!"

Uh oh. I parted the hair out of my eyes. "Yes?" I said.

"I asked you a question!" she said. "When are you going to stop living in the Human world and focus on your studies.? She sighed and moved along to the next student.

Tito looked at me and shrugged, then continued to scribble anxiously. He clearly believed everything he was told.

I slumped in my seat. Sometimes I wondered why I even bothered to try to get my Tooth Fairy Credentials. But then I remembered—Grandma Violet's story about getting trapped under a pillow on a tooth retrieval mission and the boy waking up and helping her.

Humans couldn't be all bad. There had to be some truth to Grandma's story.

See how I tried to weave the details about Gabby's appearance and personality into the story's action? I didn't stop and say, "*Gabby had dark hair and brown eyes. She was skeptical of what she was taught and was adventurous and curious.*" If I just told you these things, it would be kind of boring. We call boring sections like that *Info Dumps*, where the information about a character or the world is just dumped onto the readers, like a bucket of water. Instead of dumping your information, sprinkle your character's traits into your story, a little here, a little there.

"Just tell me what you want!"

One of the biggest things to know about your character is what they want. Each character must want something in the story, and your main character's want or need will be the driving force behind how they act and what they do. Why does Dorothy go on that long journey on the yellow brick road, end up imprisoned in a witch's castle, and drugged in a field of poppies? Because she wants to go home! If she didn't want this, she could've just kicked back with the Munchkins and had a grand ol' time. In the same way, your character's want or need is what motivates them to do everything they do and pushes the story forward. It is the force behind all their actions and choices.

In the excerpt (sample) about the fairies, can you find what Gabby wants most of all?

She wants to see what Humans are truly like. She has heard stories from her grandmother that contradict the "official" information in her school books. She wants to explore and learn. She is curious to know the truth. This is what she wants—to see the truth about Humans and to tell others that truth.

As you write, you will very likely find your main character showing you more and more about who they are and what they want. Don't be surprised if sometimes your characters decide they don't want to do what you want, and that they have their own ideas! Of course, in reality, you're making them up, but as your imagination gets going, it can feel like your characters have minds of their own!

We've explored main characters, but what about the other characters? They also need to have, to a lesser degree, an idea of what they want. And there is one kind of character in particular that you need to know very well if you hope to make them believable in your story. Do you know who they are?

Cue evil laughter…

ALSO KNOWN AS THE ANTAGONIST

WHAT MAKES A GOOD VILLAIN?

Does it sound confusing, a good villain? We don't mean a villain that is really a girl scout selling cookies who helps little old ladies across the street. Although, that could be interesting! By good, we mean a villain that feels believable and that we love to hate. Don't neglect your bad guys (and ladies). Villains, or antagonists also need to be developed. Fill out a character questionnaire and get to know them! What is it they want? World domination? A cheeseburger? Your villain needs to be active, too, always letting that deep desire fuel their choices and motivations. They should be driven and relentless in going after what they want.

Just as important as *what* your villain wants, is *why* they want it. Knowing why a villain cares about what they care about helps them become a well-rounded character. Some of our favorite villains are complicated characters with interesting pasts. Think about Voldemort, or Tom Riddle. By showing Voldemort as a young boy at Hogwarts, we feel some sympathy for him. We see the harsh conditions he grew up in, and we start to understand why he became evil. It doesn't excuse his choices or make him good, but it makes him a much more interesting character. Getting to see Draco Malfoy struggle to follow his orders for the Death Eaters makes him a stronger character.

So, how can you make your villain a little more human? Show us their weaknesses, their soft spots, and maybe a little of their past.

And remember, a villain doesn't have to be a person. A villain, or antagonist, can be lots of things. If a person or force of nature works against your main character, trying to keep them from reaching what they want, it is the antagonist of your story.

GET WRITING!

Fill out your character questionnaire on page 170.

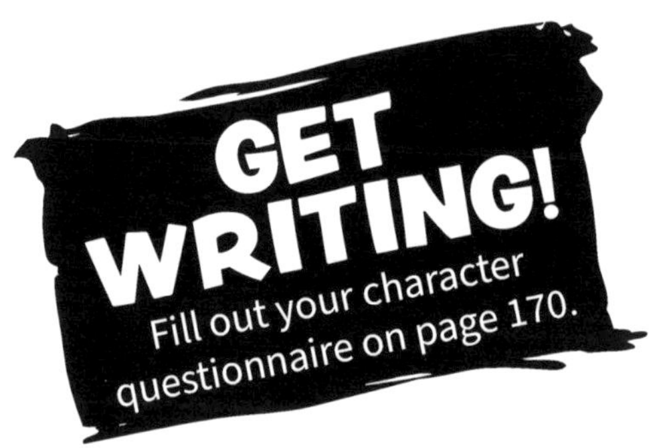

Next up, it's time to explore who will tell this tale. You might be thinking, "Um, me, obviously."

But not so fast!

What I really mean is from whose perspective, or point of view, will you tell this tale? Don't know what perspective or point of view is just yet?

Read on!

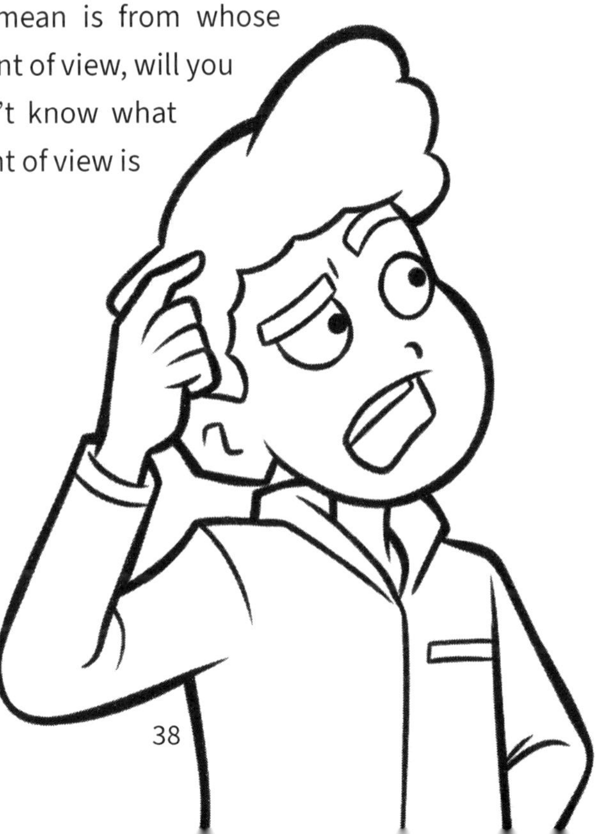

STEP 4

CHOOSE THE POINT OF VIEW (POV)

Have you ever watched a play? Have you driven to the theater, found your seat (maybe even in the front row!), and waited with excitement for the lights to dim and the curtain to go up? If you watch a play from the seats in front of the stage, you will see the stage lit up, watch the backgrounds change with different scenes, see the actors speaking to each other, and sometimes right to you. You are watching the play from the perspective, or point of view, of the audience. Point of view is where your narrator is telling the story from.

Now pretend you are not in the audience, but backstage watching from the parts of the stage that the audience can't see. This area is called "the wings." You see the stage manager rushing to make sure the actors are ready for their scenes and ready to enter the stage at the right moment. You might look up and see the backstage crew getting ready to change the background or adjusting a light. You see the audience too, if you stand just right, and you get to watch all the play's action from the sidelines. You are watching from the point of view of a stagehand.

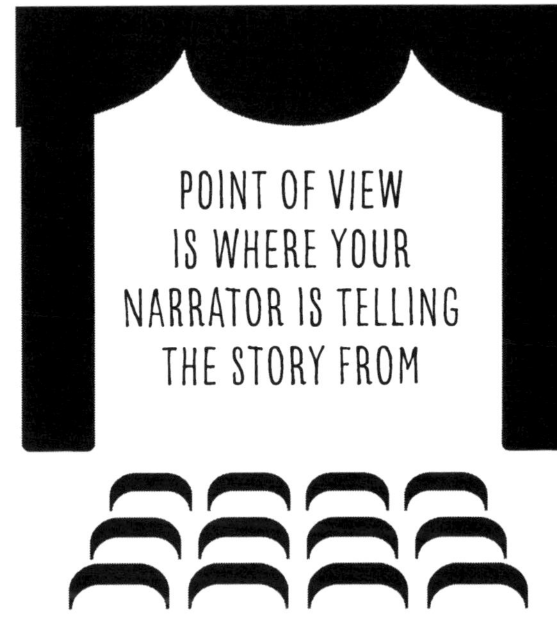

And what if you are in the play itself? You get your costume on, wait for your cue in the dark wings, then enter as your character into the brightly lit stage. You are a comical character, so you trip as you enter, and the audience laughs out loud. Then you get up, rub your seat, and proceed to act in the scene. You have practiced a lot and know your lines. You have rehearsed this scene so many times you don't even think about people watching you. You imagine yourself as your character, and for a time, you almost believe you are that clumsy guy visiting his friends. You are watching all the action from the point of view of an actor, or you could even say, from the point of view of the character.

In our example of the play, if you are the narrator, the point of view changes whether you are telling the story from the audience, backstage, or from within the play itself. The narrator is the storyteller, the voice we hear telling us the book's action, feelings, and description.

There are four points of view you can use in your novel, but we're going to stick with the three most common ones: First Person; Third Person Limited (we'll call it Third person), and Third Person Omniscient (which we'll shorten to Omniscient).

That can sound pretty confusing, but it really isn't once you get the hang of it. Every story is told from a POV. This means the narrator who is speaking is using a particular POV. Let's see how it would look in a story by using the Three Little Pigs fairy tale.

POINT OF VIEW

There are four main points of view (or POV) that you need to know in creative writing.

1 - First Person

A character, usually the main character, tells us the story. (Uses "I" throughout the story)

2 - Second Person

The narrator speaks in the third person (e.g. You opened the door.) This point of view is very rare (and difficult!)

3 - Third Person Limited

An outside narrator, not a character, tells us the story and *is limited to what **ONE CHARACTER** can see and think*. The narrator only tells the reader what that one character knows.

4 - Third Person Omniscient

An outside narrator, not a character, tells us the story and moves from one character to another. They can see and know everything. *The narrator can tell the reader the thoughts of* ***ALL THE CHARACTERS***, *not just one.*

FIRST PERSON POV

I couldn't believe my brothers were running down the road to my house! Well, actually, I could believe it because they were numskulls who thought that straw and sticks would keep a wolf away!

I was just laying the last brick on my beautiful and sturdy home when my brothers nearly crashed into me, huffing and puffing worse than, well, you know who.

Who is telling the story in this First Person POV? It is the third little pig who built the brick house. See how the story uses words like "I" instead of "he/she?" If you see the word "I" a lot, you know you are in First Person POV. But First Person is limited. We can't tell the story from this brother's perspective and then suddenly write, "The third pig was very unhappy to see his brothers at his door." Remember, the third pig is the one who is talking, and talking about yourself like you aren't yourself just feels odd.

For instance, imagine your name is Ashley. If you tell a story about eating nine pieces of pizza to your friends, you would say it like this: "I ate nine pieces of pizza in one sitting! Boy, did I have a stomach ache later on." You wouldn't say, "Ashley ate nine pieces of pizza in one sitting! Boy, did she have a stomach ache later on." If you talked about yourself like this, it would be weird, so don't do it. What POV was Ashley slipping into if she wasn't using First Person anymore? She was using Third Person.

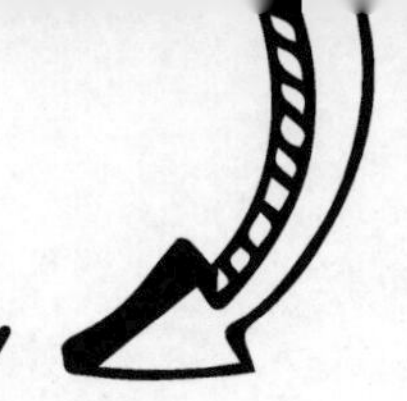

COMPARE THAT SAME SECTION OF THE THREE LITTLE PIGS TO THIS ONE.

THIRD PERSON POV

The Third pig couldn't believe his brothers were running down the road to his house! Well, actually, he could believe it because they were numskulls who thought that straw and sticks would keep a wolf away!

He was just laying the last brick on his beautiful and sturdy home, when his brothers nearly crashed into him, huffing and puffing worse than, well, you know who.

Third Person POV (He/She/They, Him/Her/Them) is the most common point of view used in novels today, followed closely by books written in First Person (I/me). When we write in this POV, we are an outside narrator telling a story. We are not a character in the book.

It gets a little tricky when we talk about Third Person versus Omniscient. But basically, Third Person means your narration is "limited" to one character, almost always your main character. We call this character the perspective character.

Imagine you are a bee on the shoulder of your main character (a honey bee, not a mean, nasty hornet!). We'll call your main character Andy. You go everywhere with Andy and can narrate, or tell us, everything he sees, hears, and even feels and thinks. If Andy isn't there, you can't tell us what someone in another room across town is talking about. You are *limited* to Andy's perspective; you see everything from Andy's point of view. If Andy doesn't see it, hear it, or feel it, you don't either. You can't tell us what his friend Jenny is feeling or thinking because you're not inside Jenny. Understand?

OMNISCIENT POV

The Third pig couldn't believe his brothers were running down the road to his house! Well, actually, he could believe it because they were numskulls who thought that straw and sticks would keep a wolf away!

Meanwhile, back at the Second pig's house, the wolf smelled the debris. He felt his stomach growl. He had almost had those pigs twice now, but they escaped each time! They would not get away a third time.

The Second pig felt like his lungs were going to explode as he ran beside his brother, but they were almost at his brother's sturdy brick house! He would never tease his brother again for being too worried about wolves, not after looking into the mouth of that wolf and seeing those sharp, pointy fangs!

It can be pretty cool to tell your story from the perspective of multiple characters. But there is a catch! You don't want your readers to feel whiplash as they whip around from one character's mind to another (this is called head-hopping, by the way). Things can get pretty muddy pretty fast if you jump all over the place. Wait, was that Jenny thinking about her cat or the villain? Was Andy feeling scared or was it his grandma? See what I mean?

To avoid head-hopping, make sure you limit yourself to one character's POV in each scene. As you jump, give us a clue whose POV you are jumping into. You could say, "Meanwhile, back at the ranch, Andy was worried about his sheep." Only don't say that because it's cheesy. Just make sure we know where we are jumping and into whose perspective, and you'll be fine.

If all of this sounds overwhelming, don't feel bad. Even experienced authors find POV pretty confusing and often make mistakes. The simplest forms are First Person (where a character is telling their own story) and Third Person Limited (where you, the narrator, stay with your main character to tell their story). Stick with one of these, and you will be on safe ground. The majority of books written today are in these two POVs.

As you read the story examples, pay attention to their POV. Each of the three stories is told from a different perspective.

Fairies in the Baseboards (page 14) is told in First Person. *Junie and Roger Get Zapped* (page 16) is told in Third Person. And *The Bully Club* (page 18) is told in Omniscient.

Once you've picked out a Point-of-View, you're ready to explore the world, or setting, of your story. After all, everything happens in a place and time, and your novel is no different. Let's learn about the world of stories!

SETTING ACTS AS THE BACKDROP TO EVERYTHING THAT HAPPENS IN YOUR STORY.

SETTING CAN BE SUCH A BIG PART OF YOUR NOVEL THAT IT MAY EVEN FEEL LIKE A CHARACTER ITSELF!

STEP 5

DECIDE ON THE SETTING

The setting in a novel, or any kind of story, is the place where everything happens. If your story is an adventure story, the setting might be a jungle in South America or a desert in Egypt. If your story is science fiction, it might be the planet XR-10. You get the picture.

Have you ever read a story where you felt confused? It might start with some engaging characters talking about cool things, but you kind of feel like everything is floating in a massive, blank background. That story didn't do a good job of showing you the setting.

When we read, our brains fill in a lot of the information and imagine the story coming to life. That is why you don't have to write your character put on his pants one leg at a time, what color they are, and that they took 15 steps from the living room to the kitchen. You can just say, "Jeff threw on some clothes and raced out of his room to see what the yelling was all about." See what I mean?

But too little information, our brains kind of hold back, waiting for the necessary facts, and don't fill anything in. This is what we call "floating heads" in creative writing, when two people are talking and we have no idea where they are or what else is going on. Nobody moves in the space, and they don't seem to have any bodies. In other words, we don't know anything about the setting.

Setting is all about the details

Just like other parts of a novel, the setting is essential to help our readers imagine the world we are creating and help them enter into the story. Imagine a movie where the whole thing took place against a blue background. Pretty boring, right?

Setting is all about the details. Details take us from a generic "jungle" to a steamy, vine-covered Amazon forest with sloths hanging from the branches. The right details help to paint the picture in your readers' minds.

But remember the "15 steps to the kitchen" from earlier? Too many details, or the *wrong* details, just bog down a story in WAY too much information. That is the recipe for your book to turn into a snooze-fest.

So how do we show our setting without making it boring? Ah-ha! We choose the *right* details. We show what is *important* to our character, and what the readers need to picture the scene, and we leave the rest behind.

Remember how our brains fill in the rest? We trust that our readers know, generally, what a jungle looks like, and we tell them a few details that show what *this* jungle looks like to *this* character in *this* mood.

An easy formula is:

A FEW CAREFULLY CHOSEN DETAILS

NOTICED BY MY CHARACTER

WHEN THEY FEEL LIKE X

SETTING

***X* stands in for whatever feeling your character is currently having: excitement, nervousness, fear, anger, etc.**

Does that sound pretty complicated? Let's look at an example from your life to make it easier to understand.

Did you ever start going to an entirely new school where you didn't know anyone? If you haven't done this, try to imagine it. You wake up, do all the everyday morning things, but in the pit of your stomach, you're worried. What will it be like? Will the kids be friendly? Who will you sit with at lunch?

As you pull up to the school and step outside, you hardly notice your mom telling you to have a nice day. Somehow your feet carry you up to the building. The doors are heavy and hard to open. You notice a group of kids goofing around in the hallway. They share exciting stories of summer vacation. You walk past them and hope to catch their eye, but they don't even notice you. You dodge kids in the busy hall, trying to find your classroom. You know where to go from the tour a few weeks ago, but as you walk you can't find it. Everything looks different, and you feel so nervous your stomach is doing flip-flops!

Now, picture a typical school morning. You wake up, a little late as usual, and rush to find clean jeans. You scarf down some cereal as Mom tries to comb your little brother's hair into something that doesn't stick straight up. You grab your backpack and head to the car. You think about finding your best friend to talk about the new Minecraft update before your teacher starts class. When you pull up, you say a quick goodbye and run into school. You notice your bag is heavy today (so much

The story changes based on how the main character feels and what they notice

homework!), and you wave to a friend. The hallway is crowded, but you know where to go. You've done this a million times.

Did you notice how the story's details changed based on how the main character felt and who was noticing them? If I had written the scene with your mom as the main character, the things she would notice would be different. We are all different people, and we go through our stories, our lives, seeing different things based on who we are.

If you struggle to know how your main character is feeling, just ask yourself, "How would I feel if this were happening to me? What would I notice or care about?" This is called writing the setting from the perspective, or view, of your character. You already know how to do this because you do it all the time. It's how you go through life every day.

Senses

As you write a scene, picture yourself as your main character, feeling what they feel. Enter into the world completely. What do you notice? What does it feel like, look like, taste like, smell like, sound like? You don't have to show your reader all the senses, but ask yourself what is important for the readers to know that will allow them to experience your world?

Look at this example from *Junie and Roger Get Zapped*. Junie has just been shocked by an electrical accident and thrown down into the grass:

> *Junie tried to lift her head from the wet grass, but it felt as heavy as a bag of dog food. Her ears rang with a high-pitched sound. What happened? Above, tiny sparks fell from the oak tree, now blackened and split.*
>
> *Junie's mind felt hazy. Sparks? A white light. Before that, Roger was chasing something. A cat? No, a squirrel, to the tree, in the rain. He barked and jumped at the tree. Junie wiggled her fingers and could feel the leash still in her hand. Before the flash of light, Roger had barked and pulled the leash. Junie turned her head. Roger! He lay motionless, but she could see his white belly rising in short breaths. She willed herself to roll to him. It was like a colossal stun gun had zapped her. But she pushed against it. She tried to talk, but her mouth didn't move. Roger! Her ears didn't hear anything. Was she even speaking, or was she deaf? She yelled in her brain, "Roger!" as she became aware of the rain trickling onto her face.*
>
> *Then, something far away and quiet. A bark! She looked at Roger, still not moving, not barking, but she heard it again. A growing bark, and then a voice. "Okay," it said. Then the word, "Squirrel?"*
>
> *Junie squinted at Roger, who opened his eyes and blinked. Staring in his deep, brown eyes, she heard the voice again. "Okay?" It sounded worried.*
>
> *Junie tried to talk but couldn't. She stared back at Roger and thought the words, "I'm okay. I just can't move."*
>
> *Roger's small tail wagged just slightly.*
>
> *Then the voice came again. "Squirrel zapped us."*

Junie suddenly remembered the thunder. She looked at the blackened tree—the sparks.

"No," she thought. "Not squirrel. Lightning."

Roger tilted his ear up. "Ouch. Not nice."

Junie tried to smile at him. Her cheeks hurt, but she did it. Her stunned muscles were now tingling, feeling less frozen.

Junie's mind, now less stunned, flipped things over and over. She was talking, with her mind. To Roger. To her dog!

In each scene, think about how your character is feeling. Imagine details that he would notice in the real world.

As you create the setting for your book, it is also important to stay consistent with your own story rules. Your story must be believable.

You may be thinking, "But my story takes place on the planet XR-10. How can that be believable? It doesn't even exist!"

Believable means that within the story world you create, you must stay consistent with your story rules. What are story rules? These are the laws that guide your world. Whenever we read the beginning of a new story, we get clues to the story world's rules. We read and learn if this is a realistic story (with similar rules to our own world), or a fantasy story (with its own rules), etc.

Remember the Rabbit Town story from earlier? If you start your story and it is evident that rabbits wear clothes, talk, and live in a town, your readers are learning this is the norm for this world. If suddenly a wild, realistic rabbit shows up, they'll be confused. If suddenly the rabbits who care about their town suddenly stop caring, that wouldn't be believable without a good reason in the story. Or if the rabbits suddenly call in the Air Force to deal with the fox, it will be unbelievable. See what I mean?

Here is an example from *The Bully Club* of how NOT to write your story. First, I will give no setting or clues to the world:

"Are you okay?" Jay asked Oliver.

"Ugh, I hate it when they do that," Oliver said, getting up.

They walked together and entered.

"One day, kids like us won't take it anymore!" Oliver said, gritting his teeth.

Jay nodded and sat down.

See how vague that feels? What happened to Oliver? Where is he getting up from? Where are they walking together and entering? Where is Jay sitting and why? So many questions distract from the story.

Now let's take a look at the same scene, with some setting and world-building included:

"Are you okay?" Jay asked Oliver, helping him out of the trash can.

"Ugh, I hate it when they do that," Oliver said, getting up and brushing the banana peel off his shoulder.

They walked together down the hallway and passed the science lab. Then they entered the double doors into the cafeteria. They were late, and most of the kids were already seated with their trays of food.

"One day, kids like us won't take it anymore!" Oliver said, gritting his teeth.

Jay nodded and sat down at a table with two girls at the far end. The girls looked at each other, then grabbed their trays and made a speedy exit.

See how easy it was to picture the setting in your mind with a few details thrown in? We learn that Oliver was shoved in a garbage can, that the boys are at school, and it is lunchtime. We also know these two boys, not just Oliver, are outcasts because the girls don't want to sit at the same table.

As you create your story settings for each scene, ask yourself where they are and what they would notice. Think about small details that can serve as clues. I didn't once have to say Oliver and Jay were on their lunch break at their middle school. And I didn't have to because you already figured that out.

What setting does your story take place in? Is it a specific town, a real place, or a more general location, like on an island or a farm? Does your story occur in contemporary times (right now) or long ago? What is the best time and place for your story to live in?

If you follow all this advice, you'll have a setting that allows your story to come alive. You'll create worlds that your characters can live in, and you won't leave everyone wondering why you're telling them that your character put on pants.

I mean, doesn't he always wear pants?! We hope so.

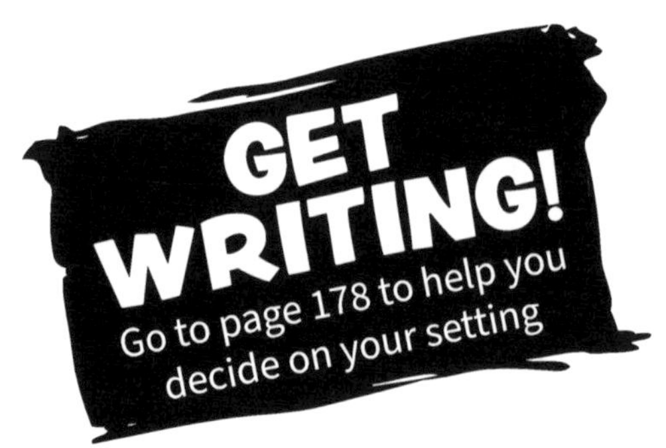

Now we know our story idea, characters, point of view, and setting for our novel. So, what could possibly be left?

Something fundamental—like what happens?! Gathering the story's events and placing them in an order that moves the story along to a satisfying end is called creating a plot.

This is what we will learn about next!

STEP 6

PLAN YOUR STORY'S PLOT

Have you ever watched a movie, say a superhero movie, and you loved it so much you rushed home as soon as it was done and told your little brother or sister everything that happened? Chances are you didn't tell *everything* that happened though—"Iron Man took a step, then he opened a door, then he turned on the light." Boring! If you did that, your little brother would never want to listen to you tell a story again.

How did you actually tell him about the movie? You told the *important* things that happened. You told the plot points—Iron Man busting out of prison and building his suit. You told the parts that were cool and important to understand the things that came next.

The plot of your novel is basically the events that happen—the choices your characters make, the betrayals, the escapes, the successes, the mistakes. These make up the plot of your story. And running like a river below the surface is what your character wants. This river connects all the events of your novel. You will keep your character going forward, trying and failing and trying again to achieve their goal. And this will repeat until one final showdown (or attempt to get what they want). If it's a happy story, your character will get it. If it's a sad story, they won't.

As we think about the events of your story and how to create your plot, it's helpful to consider some qualities of a good story.

QUALITIES OF A GOOD STORY

A story should have a clear beginning

THAT STARTS NOT TOO EARLY AND NOT TOO LATE

Aristotle (an Ancient Greek philosopher) called this starting "in media res," which means "in the midst (or middle) of things." Your story shouldn't start when your character is born if most of the action happens when they're 10. Play around with your story opening, but you usually want to find the place just a little before everything is about to change. Don't start after Dorothy is already on the yellow brick road. All novels are ultimately about the change and growth your character makes. But to see this, we have to see your character before the change and the events that cause them to change. Usually, just a little after your story starts, something should happen that causes your character to have to leave their comfortable world and go on the story's adventure. In plotting language, we often call this the Inciting Incident. In *Harry Potter*, the Inciting Incident is when Harry receives his letter and realizes he's a wizard.

A story should have conflict

Conflict is when two or more characters, or forces, want different and opposing things. For one to win, one must lose. Conflict keeps your story interesting. If the whole story is about Thanksgiving dinner that everyone makes and sits down to eat happy as clams, your readers will wonder why they should be thankful for that at all. However, if your story shows Mom lovingly cooking the turkey only to have your character's beagle get on the table and wolf it down when Mom's back is turned, now you have a story! Even better if Mom ran to the store for more cranberries and doesn't know about it yet. How will this kid get out of this problem and still save Thanksgiving?

Like in this example, the conflict and action in your plot intensifies, or gets stronger, as the story moves along. Each new problem the characters face should build off of the problem from before.

A story should have an exciting climax

The climax comes when the story's action can't build any more—something has to happen for good or bad. This is usually a big showdown with the villain (antagonist). If you don't have an actual villain, it can be when your character finally faces their fears or gets out of a final dangerous situation that the story has propelled them into.

In *Fairies in the Baseboards*, Gabby and Tito have to face the cat they ran from earlier in the story. Once the cat is defeated (with help from their human friends), the story doesn't just end there. After the climax, your story needs a settling down period—a resolution. It would feel pretty jarring if they defeat the cat, and then it was done. We would think, "But did they ever get home?"

A story should end at the right moment

The story can end when all the problems and bad guys have been dealt with, but only after the resolution. Resolution is when the main problem of the story has been resolved. At the end of a story, a little time should be taken to let the story fall back to a place where loose ends can be resolved, and we are at a new normal.

PLOTTING

As you imagine events for your novel, think about ways you can complicate your character's journey as they go after what they want. Stick your characters in situations they will struggle with. Throw up roadblocks, dead ends, and complications. Can your villain want something that runs opposite of what your main character wants? Now you have conflict.

We've already talked several times about the Three Act Structure and about breaking our one-page story foundation into three Acts. Now let's go further and see if we can create a kind of framework that we can use to order the events of our story into a plot. We can't just list a bunch of random situations and action—we have to turn it into a story by using cause and effect—building one event on another.

Plotting out your novel and ordering the events that will happen can be intimidating. At first, it sounds easy, and then you find it is like stumbling through an overgrown forest. Where is the path?

But humans have been telling stories for a very long time. People started to realize the most exciting and best-loved stories often had certain things in common. Aristotle, way back in Ancient Greece, even wrote a whole book about telling good stories! Successful stories usually follow similar patterns.

Let's take a look at a pattern that works well within the Three Act Structure. The next few pages list all the elements you need to write your novel and where to place them in your book.

ACT 1

OPENING

Here, we introduce the protagonist, or main character, and give the readers a feel for what kind of story it will be. This is also where you will offer a "hook." The hook is some interesting or intriguing scene that will catch the readers' attention, like a fish on a hook, so they won't want to put the book down.

SETUP

This section introduces the world, other important characters (such as friends or enemies) and hints at the conflict.

INCITING INCIDENT

This event launches the main events of the story. It comes as a surprise to the protagonist and could be a new problem or opportunity.

CALL TO ACTION

After the Inciting Incident, the protagonist must react within their new reality. What will the character do as a result of the Inciting Incident? What is their story goal, or the main thing they now want?

ACT 2

THE CHOICE

The protagonist makes active choices as they move forward, trying to reach their story goal.

TRY/FAIL

The protagonist and friends/sidekicks try to solve their problems. They fail a lot but have some successes as they move toward the story goal.

MIDPOINT

Some unexpected revelation sends the story in a new direction, and the stakes are raised. The protagonist may doubt, for the first time, if they can do this.

ATTACK & BAD GUYS REGROUP

The protagonist tries to keep going in try/fails, but the bad guys now see a serious threat and ramp up their attacks.

DARK MOMENT

Things are the worst they've ever been. The protagonist loses hope and nearly gives up. There seems to be no way forward.

TURNING POINT

Something offers hope (a new idea, lucky break, an unseen friend comes through). The protagonist decides to keep going.

ACT 3

A NEW PLAN

Energized by the new info or energy from the Turning Point, the protagonist forms a new plan to reach the story goal. The "team" assembles (group of friends or helpers), and everyone prepares for the final showdown to achieve the story goal.

CLIMAX

This is the biggest moment of the whole story. It is what the action has been building toward. The protagonist and team give their all to reach their goal and defeat any antagonists.

RESOLUTION

After the Climax, this is a period of resolving unfinished parts to your story and showing the protagonist living life in the new world after the antagonist has been defeated.

Story Goal

As you read ahead, you may come across the term "Story Goal." Essentially, the story goal is the main thing your protagonist (main character) wants in the story. Your character may want lots of things, but you should be able to figure out the main thing they want. Dorothy wants to get to the wizard, and she wants to help her friends, and she wants to keep Toto safe, but her most significant want? That is easy—she wants to go home! Often, your character's lesser wants are actually small steps toward the big thing they want. Whatever that "big thing" is, that is your character's story goal.

Let's look at an example of a story plotted out to include all these parts or elements. In the following pages, I have filled in a plotting worksheet with the plot of *The Bully Club*. Read over the sections and see how the plot points fit with each part of the story.

ACT 1

THE BEGINNING

MAJOR PLOT POINTS

OPENING

The opening introduces the protagonist or main character, gives the readers a feel for what kind of story it will be, and offers a "hook."

We meet Oliver after he has just been thrown in the trash can. Oliver is skinny, looks younger than he is, and is angry about being picked on all the time.

SETUP

This section introduces the world, other important characters (such as friends or enemies), and hints at the conflict.

We get to meet Jay, who is chubby and not good at sports. A new boy, Brayden, shows up and is made lab partners with Jay. Brayden looks cool but is picked on too because he's new.

INCITING INCIDENT

This event launches the main events of the story. It comes as a surprise to the protagonist and could be a new problem or opportunity.

When some bullies go too far and embarrass Oliver in front of Hailey (the girl he likes), he snaps inside. Something has to change!

CALL TO ACTION

After the Inciting Incident, the protagonist must react to the new reality. What will the character do as a result of the Inciting Incident?

Oliver sees a bunch of soccer players hanging out and realizes safety comes in numbers. He has a vision to create a "Bully Club," a group for bullied kids to join together and find safety and confidence in numbers.

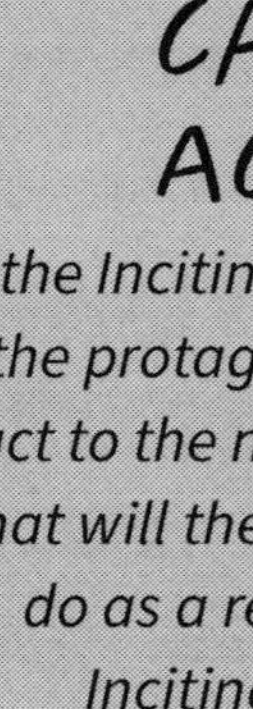

ACT 2

THE MIDDLE

PART 1

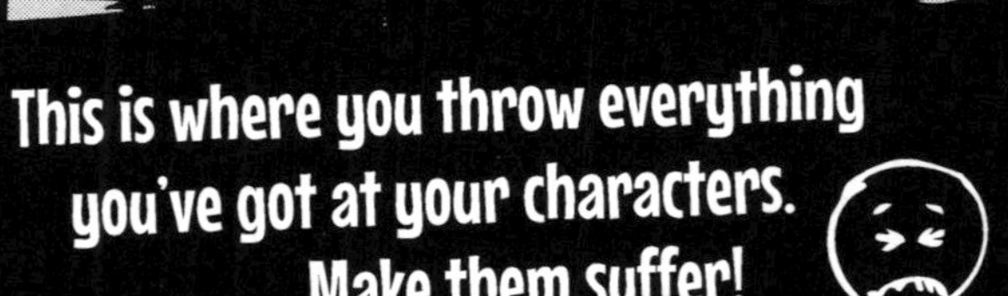

THE CHOICE

The protagonist makes active choices as they move forward, trying to reach their story goal.

MAJOR PLOT POINTS

Oliver starts recruiting other kids who have been bullied to join the Bully Club. Jay and Brayden become co-leaders with Oliver. The kids enjoy the companionship and grow less afraid.

TRY/FAIL

The protagonist and friends/sidekicks try to solve their problems. They fail a lot, but have some successes as they move toward the story goal.

The group members stand up to bullies. At first, they're encouraged by seeing the bullies back down, but soon the bullies regroup, and the backlash is almost worse than before. Some kids decide to quit the Club, but many kids feel a new sense of confidence, even with the setbacks. Brayden becomes secret friends with two of the bullies. Oliver goes on the offensive. He even picks on a couple of bullies!

MIDPOINT/ REVERSAL

Some unexpected revelation sends the story in a new direction, and the stakes are raised. The protagonist may doubt if they can really do this.

Things seem to go well until Oliver goes too far and the bullies complain to the vice-principal that they are being bullied! The vice-principal sides with them, and the Bully Club is forced to disband. There is infighting among Oliver, Jay, and Brayden.

ACT 2

PART 2

RIGHT **AFTER** THE MIDDLE

You've thrown so many obstacles and challenges at your hero, they don't know if they can go on.

ATTACK & BAD GUYS REGROUP

The protagonist tries to keep going in try/fails, but the bad guys now see a serious threat and ramp up their attacks.

MAJOR PLOT POINTS

Some kids are up for meeting anyways,
but some are afraid to disobey the vice-principal.

The bullies seem worse than ever.

Dark Moment

Things are the worst they've ever been. The protagonist loses hope and nearly gives up. There seems to be no way forward.

They find out Brayden has been friends with two of the bullies all along. Oliver is livid. After one ruthless retaliation against a younger bully, Brayden quits. Jay is unsure, and Oliver is very discouraged and almost gives up the idea altogether.
He questions who he really is and realizes he has become a bully himself—the one thing he hates most of all.

Turning Point

Something offers hope (a new idea, lucky break, an unseen friend comes through). The protagonist decides to keep going.

Oliver is sick of being a bully, but also sick of being bullied himself. How can he end this once and for all? Jay tells Oliver he has been put in charge of equipment for the upcoming field day. Oliver has an idea.

ACT 3

END

With the climax and the resolution, the third act leaves the protagonist and other characters with a new understanding of who they really are.

A NEW PLAN

The protagonist forms a new plan to reach the story goal, energized by the new info or energy from the Turning Point.

MAJOR PLOT POINTS

Field day is coming up, with a "Club Olympics." The three worst bullies of the school form a team. Oliver creates a new club through the school office so they can take part in the field day. Oliver makes amends with Brayden, and the two of them, with Jay, form a team. Oliver shares his idea to rig the bullies' equipment so that they will struggle at each event. He reassures Brayden it isn't to tease them. Oliver wants the chance to show kindness to the bullies, especially during an opportunity that could be used to tease and harass them.

CLIMAX

This is the biggest moment of the whole story. It's what the action has been building toward. The protagonist and team give their all to reach their goal and defeat any antagonists.

The club teams are pitted against each other as the Club Olympics start. Jay makes sure the bullies have the sabotaged gear, and event after event, they lose. The bullies are humbled and embarrassed. But instead of teasing, Oliver, Jay, and Brayden are kind to them.

RESOLUTION

After the Climax, this is a period of resolving unfinished parts to your story and showing the protagonist living life in the new world after the antagonist has been defeated.

Oliver disbands the Bully Club. He decides instead to make a hobby club that focuses on positive things, sharing and exploring the kids' interests in the group. Oliver gets up the nerve to ask Hailey to come to a meeting, and she agrees. One of the former worst bullies of the school even decides to join, as do the two friends Brayden made. Oliver looks around the room during the new club's first meeting and smiles. He's created a group where everyone is welcome.

Now that you have a good idea of how plot points and story elements work in a novel, you are ready to plot out your book! Take your one-page story version of your book and try your hand at filling out the worksheet at the back of the book (page 180).

As you fill it out, remember it doesn't have to be just right from the get-go. Play around with different ideas! This is brainstorming time. Should your Inciting Incident be when the gnome learns who his father *really* is? Or when a bad case of bed bugs strikes his village? The possibilities are endless. Have fun and see what you come up with!

FOLLOWING THIS 3 ACT STRUCTURE IS A GOOD WAY TO PLOT YOUR NOVEL WHEN YOU'RE FIRST STARTING OUT, BUT...

YOU DON'T HAVE TO FOLLOW THIS FORMAT (OR ANYONE ELSE'S)! YOU'RE THE AUTHOR OF YOUR BOOK AND YOU GET TO MAKE YOUR OWN RULES!

STEP 7

DIVIDE YOUR PLOT INTO CHAPTERS

With the major plot points of your novel figured out, it is time to develop your story further. After all, most long stories have more than one story going on. That may seem confusing, but think about it. There are hints of other minor plots, or sub-plots, right there in the plot worksheet for *The Bully Club*.

A subplot is a side story that is going on at the same time as the main story. Go ahead, flip back and see if you can find the hints of side stories in the plot of *The Bully Club*.

Did you find any? Here are the subplots I see:

Oliver and Hailey

Oliver has a crush on Hailey but is embarrassed in front of her by the bullies. He fails at his attempts to impress her and get her attention.

Brayden and his two new friends

Brayden becomes friends with two minor bully characters, which causes strife later on with Oliver.

Did you also notice how these subplots are resolved by the end of the story? In the Hailey subplot, Oliver starts off too embarrassed to talk to her, but by the end of the story, his confidence has grown enough to ask her to join his club.

With Brayden and his friends, he is able to remain friends with both Oliver and Jay *and* the two former bullies. Brayden even manages to get his friends to join Oliver's new club, and he doesn't have to worry about his people in the group not accepting each other anymore.

Developing your story with subplots

There is a reason we say subplots *develop* a story, but we don't say subplots are *slapped onto* a story. The subplots should naturally grow, or develop, out of your main storyline. They should become such a significant part of your main story tree that the story would suffer and maybe even die if we cut them off.

This is not the case with slapped-on subplots. These are small storylines that are like boards pounded onto a tree to make a tree house. We can remove them and the tree won't be affected by it. As a matter of fact, if we remove them, the tree may even thank us and be better off for it!

If I slapped on a subplot that Oliver's dog was missing and had nothing to do with the main plot about bullying, it would be an unnecessary subplot weighing down the whole novel. If I genuinely liked my subplot, I could try to make it necessary to the main plot. Perhaps one of the bullies takes Oliver's dog as a prank, leading to his Dark Moment in the plot. In that case, the missing dog subplot could become another branch on the tree of our story and even a main branch that other interesting ideas could grow off of.

If you try taking a subplot out of the novel and the story suffers, you know it's a good subplot!

The point is to make sure your subplots grow out of your story naturally. Take a look at the plot worksheet you filled out. Do you see any subplots trying to peek out? Are there any areas you can develop in your story?

If you're having trouble finding subplots, think about *why* your character wants what they want as their story goal. Is there another story hiding beneath the main one? What about your side characters? What do they want, and why are they going along on the story journey? What about your antagonist and bad guys? What are their motivations? As you think and play with your story, don't be surprised if mini-stories bloom forward, all fighting for a chance to have their moment in the sun! You may find that you have too many subplots before long! For a short novel, a good rule is one or two, but not too many to distract from your main storyline.

Dividing your story into chapters and scenes

I know what you must be thinking. "I've figured out my plot points, and a few ideas for subplots, but just how in the world do I turn that into chapters and scenes and an actual novel with 40,000 words?!"

Or maybe you're just thinking you want a cheeseburger.

At any rate, the good news is you don't have to write it all at once. Just like Rome wasn't built in a day, your novel doesn't have to happen in one sitting. People figured out long ago, with such a long story, we need breaks, divisions, ways to manage a narrative this big and help it stay structured.

If you've read a novel or book with chapters, you are already aware of some of the ways long stories are structured: they have Acts (which you've already learned about), and they have chapters, and they have scenes within the chapters.

So, how long should an Act be, a Chapter, a Scene? A little math can help us figure out how long, or how many words, each section of your novel should be. Ideally, your first Act should be about 25% of your total book. This is the same for your third Act (25% as well). That means, math drum roll, please, your second Act should be 50% of your book.

So, if your entire novel is 40,000 words, and each chapter is around 1,000 words, we can figure out how to divide up your book with a bit of math magic.

If you know you will have around 40,000 words for your novel, and each chapter will be about 1,000 words, your book will have 40 chapters, right?

ACTS

Acts are one way to name the major sections of a novel. Unlike chapters, Acts usually aren't obvious—they don't have special headings and don't show up in the Table of Contents. You've been plotting your story with the Three Act Structure in the worksheets.

CHAPTERS

Acts are broken up into several chapters. You know all those plot points like the Midpoint and the Dark Moment? Those will happen in chapters, sometimes in one, and sometimes over many.

SCENES

Chapters are broken up into scenes, and you'll usually see two to four in one chapter. When you're reading a chapter and the story goes to a new location, place in time, or changes point of view, that usually means a new scene has started.

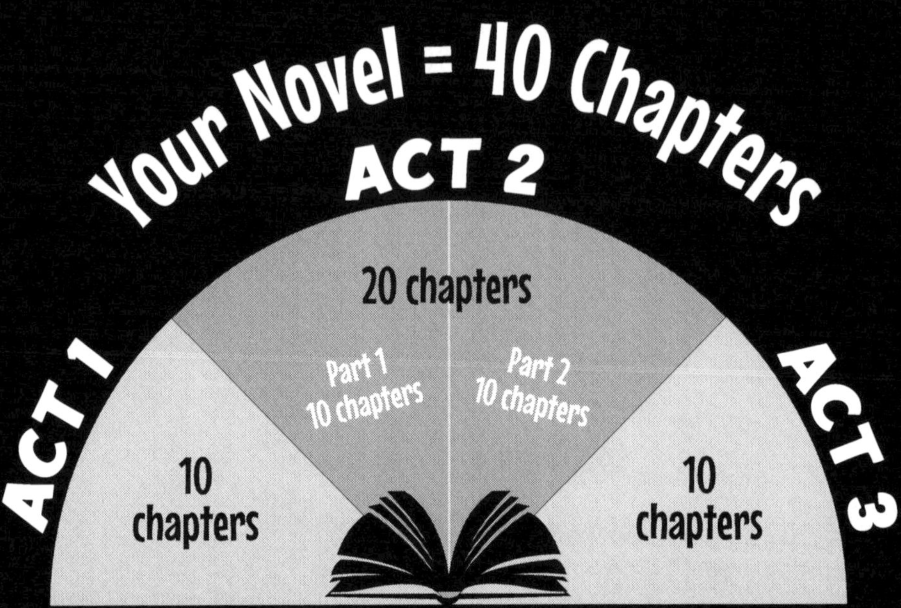

ACT 1 = 10 CHAPTERS

25% of 40 chapters = 10 chapters

ACT 2 = 20 CHAPTERS

50% of 40 chapters = 20 chapters

ACT 3 = 10 CHAPTERS

25% of 40 chapters = 10 chapters

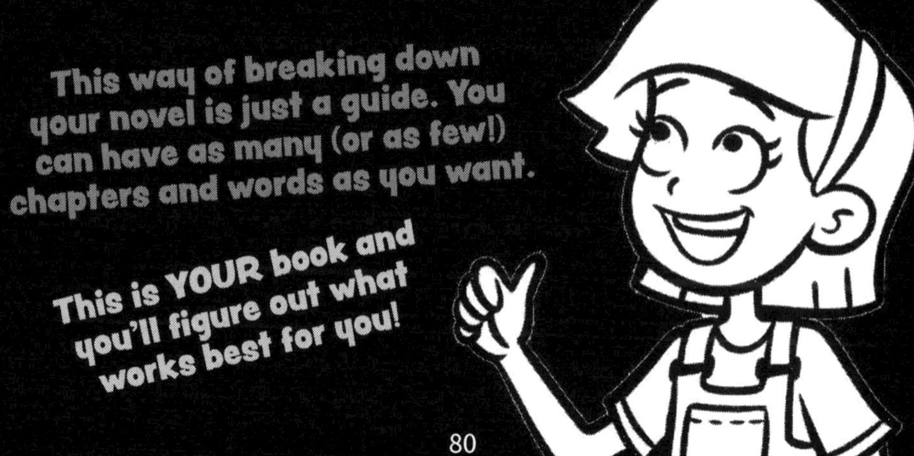

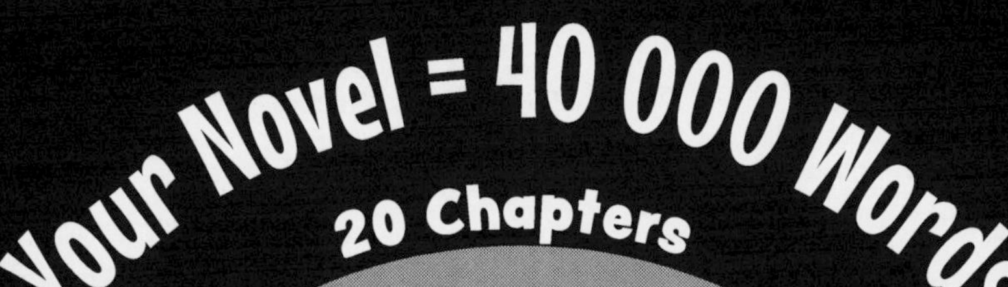

20 Chapters

10 Chapters

THE MIDDLE AND RIGHT AFTER THE MIDDLE

10 Chapters

THE BEGINNING

THE END

CHAPTER = 1000 WORDS

CHAPTER = 2 TO 4 SCENES

40,000 words = 100 to 150 pages IN A PRINTED BOOK

40,000 words = 80 pages (give or take) IN SINGLE-SPACED TYPED 8.5 X 11 SHEETS

THE LION, THE WITCH, AND THE WARDROBE = 38,421 WORDS

CHARLIE AND THE CHOCOLATE FACTORY = 30,644 WORDS

SOME GOOD ADVICE ON WHEN TO END A CHAPTER

When the scenes have finished for that section

If you've resolved one mini-problem and are starting on a new part, that may be an appropriate place to end your chapter.

When you've reached your word count for the chapter

If you are trying to make each chapter around 1,000 words, and you are at 950 words and could go into a whole new scene, end your chapter and start the next section in a new one. If you only have 250 words and need to go to a new scene, you can just drop down two lines (hit enter twice) and start your new scene without ending the chapter.

When you've just finished some exciting moment

Ending a chapter on a cliffhanger, or when your readers can't wait to see what happens next, is one way to make sure your readers move forward in your book. Chapters are natural places for readers to put down the book to take a break, go to sleep, etc. If you end your chapter in an exciting spot where something has just been revealed, it can help ensure your readers will actually come back and not forget about your book entirely. Just be careful not to do this all the time. Too many cliffhangers in a book can start to feel annoying.

Because we start as readers, most writers already have a built-in sense of where chapters should end. Above all, trust yourself as you tell your story and come to the natural pauses.

Now you know that all the action of Act 1 needs to take part in 10 chapters. Let's look at the plot worksheet for Act 1 of *The Bully Club* again, and I'll add chapter breaks.

ACT 1

THE BEGINNING

MAJOR PLOT POINTS

OPENING

The opening introduces the protagonist or main character, gives the readers a feel for what kind of story it will be, and offers a "hook."

[Chapter 1] We meet Oliver after he has just been thrown in the trash can. Oliver is skinny, looks younger than he is, and is angry about being picked on all the time.

SETUP

This section introduces the world, other important characters (such as friends or enemies), and hints at the conflict.

[Chapter 2] We get to meet Jay, who is chubby and not good at sports. A new boy, Brayden, shows up and is made lab partners with Jay. Brayden looks cool but is picked on too because he's new.

INCITING INCIDENT

This event launches the main events of the story. It comes as a surprise to the protagonist and could be a new problem or opportunity.

[Chapter 5-6] When some bullies go too far and embarrass Oliver in front of Hailey (the girl he likes), he snaps inside. Something has to change!

[Chapter 7-8] Oliver and others continue to suffer under the bullies. New minor characters are introduced, and we get to know the bullies more.

CALL TO ACTION

After the Inciting Incident, the protagonist must react to the new reality. What will the character do as a result of the Inciting Incident?

[Chapter 9-10] Oliver sees a bunch of soccer players hanging out and realizes safety comes in numbers. He has a vision to create a "Bully Club," a group for bullied kids to join together and find safety and confidence in numbers.

Notice how the plot points, such as the Call to Action and Setup, may contain multiple chapters, not just one. These plot points are not the ONLY things that happen in your novel, but they need to occur roughly in this order and in the Act they are shown in. So basically, you will have other fun, and character-building things happen in your novel that may not be a plot point.

Go ahead and try to create a chapter outline for your novel now. Using your plot worksheet from the back of the book, figure out where your chapters will go (remembering that you can always make changes later on). Make a list with each chapter and a short sentence or two about what will happen in that chapter.

This outline will help keep you on track as you begin to write your book. If you are itching to get going on your novel, go ahead! You don't even have to write chapters in order. Feel like jumping into chapter five with your big fight scene? You can do it! Some authors work this way, and some even write the end first!

Personally, I like to go in order because it helps me build my characters. I can see them grow as they journey toward their goals. But, if I have a vision for a great piece of dialogue (conversation) that takes place later on, I will jot that down and save it.

You can write with pen and paper, pencil and paper, or type your first draft on the computer. Writers do any and all of these things. Remember, this is all advice and guidance, but you are the writer, and you can, and will, find a way that you like to write and create stories. There are published authors who don't make an outline at all! They dive in and write by the seat of their pants. Others may take pages and pages of notes, detailing and outlining exactly how their novel will take shape. Neither way is wrong or best!

In this book, we guide you through creating an outline because it is easy for new writers to get way off track and lose their way in the story. When that happens, they're tempted to give up. We don't want that to happen! Plus, it is easier to start with a plan, even a simple one, rather than try to make sense of a bunch of writing that goes all over the place.

Next, let's look at how to create scenes and chapters that keep your readers engaged and excited to see what comes next.

How do you do that?

By creating a story with action and suspense!

SET UP SOME ACTION

Do you remember way back in step five when we talked about setting and described the kid who put on his pants one leg at time, and then took 15 steps to the kitchen?

We described a story that had action, but the speed of that action, the pacing, was super slow. Pacing is basically how fast or slow the story unfolds. Why is it important? It can mean the difference between a story that keeps your readers interested and one that doesn't.

Let's look at a couple of common problems that new writers have with pacing.

THE PACING IS TOO S...L...O...W

If your pacing is too slow, your story will feel like a snail is telling it. Stories with slow pacing issues are boring and make you start wondering if you might instead prefer to do your homework than keep reading.

So, what are some reasons a story might slow down to snail speed?

Too much description

This is a big one. If you describe putting on pants in great detail—like earlier—you slow down the story's action. Here is an example from *The Bully Club* of a section that is written with too much description. It comes from the beginning of Act II, where Oliver starts recruiting other kids to join his new club:

> *Oliver stepped through the door into the cafeteria. He looked around the room. A group of soccer players were over at the foosball tables. Oliver recognized them as Terrence, Jacob, and Scott. They were also in his math class. It looked like Scott had just won the game since he was doing a victory dance.*
>
> *Oliver had never played foosball, although he wanted to. But a kid like him didn't just walk up to kids like that and say, "Hey, can I play?"*
>
> *Oliver noticed a group of girls laughing at a full table. He had never sat at a full table before. Oh well, he thought.*
>
> *He glanced around at the kids lining up for the Tuesday Meatloaf special. Some kids had Jell-O on their trays, and some didn't. Oliver couldn't stand Jell-O and the way it jiggled like Jaba the Hutt. He always chose the cookie instead.*

Then he noticed Derek. He walked over the square-tiled floor, avoiding a spot where someone had dropped some meatloaf. He stood next to a long table with only one kid at it.

Derek looked up at him, then back at his plate. "Yeah?" he said.

Oliver walked to the other side of the table and put one foot into the bench, then another as he sat down. He placed his hands on the table. "I'm here to talk," he said.

Okay, enough! Is that boring, or what! This paragraph shows Oliver going to the cafeteria to recruit other kids, but it is WAY bogged down in too many details that don't matter.

Do we need to know the boys' names playing foosball or that they are in Oliver's math class? Um, no.

Do we need to hear a whole section on why Oliver doesn't like Jello-O? Nope.

Look how the scene's action became slowed down under all these extra details.

Here is another go at it, still full of description, but the *right* description:

Oliver stepped into the cafeteria, full of the usual chaos of lunch break—foosball, a group of girls laughing, the hum of a million conversations going on. It was an ordinary day. Only today, instead of waiting in line for the Tuesday meatloaf special, he was scanning the room for one particular thing. Usually, Oliver checked the room to avoid bullies, but now he looked for something different. He was looking for the kids who sat alone, the kids who picked at their sandwiches while darting nervous glances over their shoulder.

We still set the scene of a busy middle school cafeteria, but with just a few details: foosball, girl laughing, conversations, meatloaf. Then, we get on to the point of the whole scene, which is Oliver finding kids to recruit to his new club.

Long sentences and paragraphs

Another way pacing is slowed down is by long sentences and paragraphs that go on and on, especially about one thing. Take a look at how I make this sentence even worse from the "too much description" section above. I've added in even more descriptions and adjectives to weigh it down:

Then he noticed Derek, who had dark curly hair and was wearing an orange polo shirt and picking at his peanut butter and jelly sandwich. He walked over the shiny square-tiled floor, trying not to slip and avoiding a spot where someone had dropped some meatloaf in a big gloppy mess, and stood next to a long brown table with only Derek sitting at it.

The second sentence is 41 words! And so much of it is unnecessary. Instead of just saying "Oliver walked over to Derek" in five words, we describe everything under the sun so that Oliver has to slog through adjective after adjective just to get to Derek. We're in danger of him, and the readers, giving up!

Too much backstory

This may be the number one reason stories by new writers go too slow. Backstory is when you stop the forward action of the story to explain something from the past, or sometimes write a flashback to show a scene from earlier.

Why does this slow a story down? The answer is right there in my definition of backstory—"when you stop the forward action of the story." Think of it like biking over to your friend's house on the next street over. You can go directly there, or you can bike a little bit, then go back for your Pokémon cards, get on your bike again, then stop because your hat flew off, get going again, only to remember you forgot to shut the gate and your dog might follow you. This is just like backstory. It may be important to get your Pokémon cards and your hat, but if you do that, it will slow you down from getting where you want to go.

Backstory can be used, but be careful. Because if you go backward, it will slow down your story's momentum and take longer to get where you want to go.

Too many subplots

Now, don't get me wrong, subplots are great for adding depth to your story and developing characters, but they can slow things down if you have too many. Remember when we said one or two subplots was a good number? That's a good guide. In *The Bully Club,* we could go off and talk about the lunch lady who made the meatloaf on Tuesdays. We could even show Oliver having a relationship with her and her being kind to him when he got put in the trash can. Maybe this would be an excellent subplot to build up and be fun to write about, but if it doesn't have much to do with the main plot, it might just slow things down.

Be careful of subplots springing up all over the place. As you get into your novel and your creativity takes flight, sometimes you have to rein it in a little. A phrase writers say is, "Kill your darlings." What does this mean?! It means that sometimes you love something in your book, like a subplot, but if it doesn't help the book to be better, you should cut it out. It can be painful! But don't be afraid to make cuts. You can save the things you cut for another project someday. And nobody wants to read a book that is sailing along trying to drag fifteen subplots behind it covered in barnacles and seaweed. Cut off the dead weight and let your book soar!

Too much time in your character's head

Letting us see into your character's thoughts and feelings help readers connect with your main character. But too much time stuck inside your character means the outside action has to slow down, or worse, stop altogether. The novel's action—the *what happens next* and *what happens after that*—is what keeps us turning pages and staying up past our bedtime. While it's fantastic to get a glimpse inside someone else's mind, remember to keep these glimpses short and use them sparingly—and only when relevant.

Let me clarify something. A section of your book with a slower pace is not necessarily a bad thing. Even the most action-packed books, such as thrillers, throw in downtimes and chapters where the characters are researching or catching their breath. Why? Because just boom, boom, boom, constant action is tiring. Pay attention the next time you watch an action movie and try to spot the slower places. These are designed to give the characters, and you, a chance to slow down and process all the action before moving ahead. A fast-paced scene can be exciting, but too many in a row become exhausting.

So, is a long paragraph wrong? No. Sometimes you want to draw attention to something important that your readers need to pay attention to. If you purposefully slow down the pace to highlight a scene or detail, that's fine. You just want to make sure you have variety in your book, and it isn't all slow or all fast.

Now that we know what slows down the action, what techniques can we use to change the pace?

SPEED IT UP

Using strong active verbs

What do I mean by strong verbs? How can a verb be weak?

Remember, a verb describes an action and what the characters are doing, feeling, etc. One way a verb can be weak is it isn't specific. I could say, "Oliver walked into the room." There is nothing wrong with that, but I just missed an easy opportunity to show something in a more precise way. This sentence doesn't tell me several things: how Oliver walked (fast, slow, clumsily) or how he's feeling (happy, sad, tired).

Some people will tack on an adverb to the verb, which tells *how* the action was performed. If I did this, I could say, "Oliver walked (verb) quickly (adverb) into the room." This gives us more information, but I'm still using the relatively weak verb "walked." Is there a more robust, more precise way to say how Oliver walked? If I pull out my thesaurus, I can see there are a whole lot of other words to say "walked" that carry more meaning with them—sauntered, dashed, strolled, zoomed, bounced, crashed, meandered, etc.

If I want to speed up the action of my scene, I could use verbs that carry that sense of speed.

Here is a re-write of the above scene where Oliver recruits other kids to his club. I'm focusing on eliminating unnecessary details and including active verbs (which I have highlighted in bold):

> *Oliver* **burst** *into the room and* **zoomed** *in on Derek, who was sitting alone with his milk carton.*
>
> *Derek looked up, confused.*
>
> *"Hey, I'm Oliver. Do you get bullied?"*
>
> *Derek's glance* **darted** *around the room. "No!"*
>
> *Oliver* **slammed** *his hand on the table. "Look, I'm not here to make fun of you! Just read this." He flicked a small folded paper across the table.*
>
> *Derek* **grabbed** *it. "What is it?"*
>
> *Oliver* **jumped** *up, smiling. "It's your ticket to freedom."*

Did you notice the active verbs like "burst" and "grabbed?" Suddenly we get a clearer image of how Oliver came into that room—like a man on a mission with no time to waste. Even the exclamation marks in Oliver's speech add to the urgency. He is recruiting for his club, and he can't wait to give every bullied kid the power that belonging to a group can offer.

More Dialogue

What is dialogue? It's the parts of the book where characters talk. Another trick to quicken the pace of a scene is to limit the narration (where you are describing the action, etc.) and give more dialogue.

This is precisely what I did in the scene above from *The Bully Club*. Most of the scene is dialogue and action happening while the characters are speaking. Besides the scene feeling faster because the characters are talking, there are other reasons it helps with the pacing. A lot of dialogue naturally makes the scene read faster because there are fewer words to wade through. The readers also turn pages quicker because you jump to a new line with each person talking and can't fit as many words on a page.

Short sentences

Short sentences clip along quickly as your readers go through your book. Longer, complicated sentences take more effort and time to sort through. Does this mean you should have every sentence short?

The cat ran. The boy chased it. "Help!" called the woman. "Save my cat." The policeman helped too.

Please, no. That would read like a book for early readers! Longer sentences add sophistication to your writing. A variety of short and long helps to keep your sentences from being boring.

But if you're writing a scene that you want to be fast-paced, focus on shorter sentences as a rule. If you have your main character in a chase scene with the villain, don't have them stop and give a long speech. If you are running, the most you might get out is a single word or two like "stop" or "that way!"

In the earlier example about Oliver, the majority of his dialogue has three to five words per sentence, tops.

Think about "stakes" and insert a time bomb

Okay, no, not literally. It wouldn't make much sense if your story is about gnomes and their peaceful forest life, and a squirrel shows up with a time bomb. What I mean is to provide some reason your characters can't take forever to solve their problems. This is called a "time bomb." In some stories, it might be a literal time bomb that goes off in 24 hours and means your detective has to solve the clues or else. But whatever the mechanism is that puts your characters in a time crunch, doing so will quicken the pace and force things in your story to happen quickly.

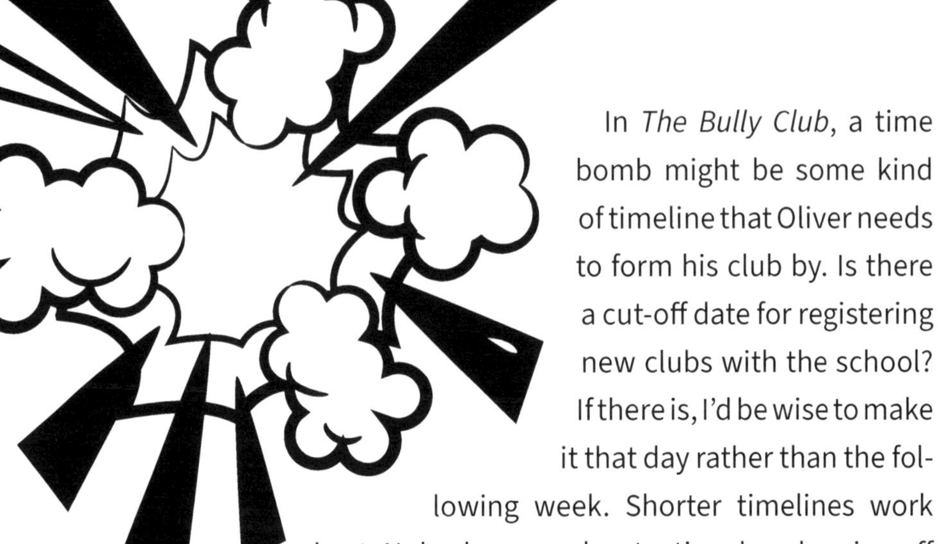

In *The Bully Club*, a time bomb might be some kind of timeline that Oliver needs to form his club by. Is there a cut-off date for registering new clubs with the school? If there is, I'd be wise to make it that day rather than the following week. Shorter timelines work best. Nobody cares about a time bomb going off next month. Yawn. But a time bomb going off in two hours? Now you have my attention. Inserting a time bomb into your plot adds drama and makes your readers care about what is at stake. If nothing is at stake—no one will lose anything or gain anything by what is happening—a story just isn't very interesting. So, whenever possible, raise the stakes for your characters. They don't have to be life or death stakes, like with a literal time bomb, but just make sure it feels absolutely crucial to your characters. If Oliver doesn't form a club then his life continues as before, becoming intolerable. He is willing to do all kinds of things to make his circumstances change for the better. To him, there is a lot at stake.

Use Cliffhangers

We've all been there. You are reading a book, it is already after midnight, and your eyes keep falling closed, but you just don't want to put the book down! You just have to find out what comes next.

Cliffhangers are where you leave something "hanging" at the end of the chapter—sometimes it's your main character hanging off a cliff, but usually it's some critical piece of information that is hinted at but not revealed. By setting up these mini-mysteries, you keep your readers eager to flip on to the next chapter.

If you have a section of your book that is slow, try inserting a few of these. Are you ending your chapters at an exciting place, or when everything is "back to normal?" Try to switch it up and see what happens if you end your chapter right as something is revealed or about to be. Even revelations can be cliffhangers if you tell us some new information, but the main character's reaction to it hasn't been revealed yet. Chances are we'll flip ahead because we can't wait to see what they'll do with the new information or how they will feel about it.

GET WRITING!

Go to page 196 and list some action scenes and events

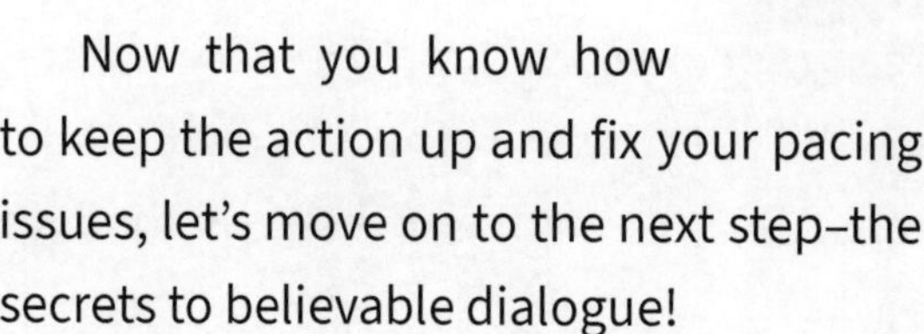

Now that you know how to keep the action up and fix your pacing issues, let's move on to the next step–the secrets to believable dialogue!

STEP 9

WRITE GREAT DIALOGUE

Dialogue is the part of the story where your characters get to talk! Of course, if you're using the first-person point of view, your characters are already speaking through the story's narration. However, there are still parts where other characters talk, and your main character speaks to them. This is shown through dialogue.

There is a proper way to punctuate and format dialogue to clarify who is speaking and the meaning of what they are saying. This is the way all dialogue is written in published books. Your readers will be used to these rules and will be confused if you don't follow them. The last thing we want is confused readers who throw your book across the room in a fit of frustration.

DIALOGUE GUIDELINES

Jump to a new line with every speaker

Every time a new character speaks, jump to a new line. Jenny can ramble on and on, and I don't need to start a new paragraph. But the moment Albert decides to speak or even do something (such as nod his head, get up and leave, etc.), I need to show that with a new paragraph. New paragraphs help the reader keep track of who is talking.

Use dialogue tags and actions to tell who is speaking

By including the simple words "he said" or "Jenny said," you help your readers keep everyone straight. These are called dialogue tags. However, you can also do this with short action sentences. If Jenny coughs, and then a new line of dialogue starts on the same line, the readers will assume it is Jenny, and you don't have to end it with, "Jenny said."

Avoid talking heads! Add action to the conversation!

Action sentences are a nice trick because you can avoid using the word "said" all the time, plus you get to tell us what someone is doing and prevent the sensation of talking heads. Remember talking heads? People talk but don't seem to be anywhere or be doing anything with their bodies. Including little actions help the reader see the scene better in their minds and keep the characters grounded in action.

ASIDE NOTE

While the occasional use of other dialogue tags beyond "she said/he said/they said" is okay, don't overdo it. You can use a "whispered" or "exclaimed," but avoid a bunch of unnecessary tags that describe too much. Ideally, your actual dialogue—what is being said—should convey how it is said. If it isn't apparent through the words and punctuation, such as a question mark or exclamation mark, then using an "asked" or "yelled" is okay.

Quotation marks only go around speech

If someone is saying it, it needs to be in quotation marks.

We don't write:

We write:

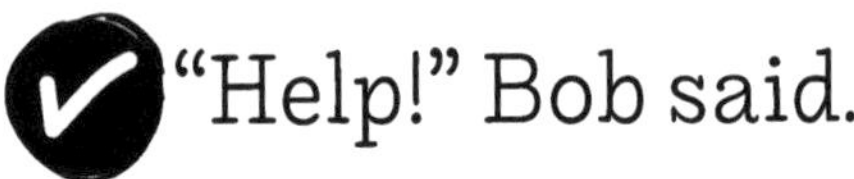

The thing that Bob is saying (Help!) goes inside quotation marks. We DON'T put the quotation marks around "Bob said" as well, because Bob isn't saying the words, "Bob said."

Punctuation goes inside the quotation marks

Punctuation refers to periods, commas, question marks, exclamation marks. All of these go inside of the quotations in the sentence.

So, we don't write:

 "Help"! Bob said. "My cat is lost".

We write:

 "Help!" Bob said. "My cat is lost."

See how the quotations give a friendly little hug to the sentence that is being spoken? Make sure the punctuation marks get the hug too, and aren't left out in the cold.

Sometimes periods need to be commas

That's right. This sounds like a weird rule, but let me explain.

A spoken sentence like this:

"The milk is on aisle five."

has a period.

But when you add a dialogue tag after that sentence, like this:

"The milk is on aisle five," said the grocery clerk.

you put a comma instead of a period.

Because that sentence ends with a period (it doesn't end in an exclamation point or a question mark)—**and** has a dialogue tag after it—such as said the grocery clerk—we ***replace*** the period with a comma.

Here is a simple formula to remember:

SPOKEN WORDS

Example: **"I'm cold."**

DIALOGUE TAG

Example: **he said.**

CHANGE PERIOD TO COMMA

"I'm cold," he said.

Everyone knows the period goes at the end of the sentence, and now the spoken words and the dialogue tag are considered the full sentence.

Dialogue tags are never capitalized

A dialogue tag following a sentence is NEVER capitalized, even if we use other punctuation.

This would be wrong:

✗ "The milk is on aisle five." Said the grocery clerk.

This is the correct way:

✓ "The milk is on aisle five," said the grocery clerk.

Notice how "said" is NOT capitalized.

Here it is with different punctuation:

✓ "The milk is on aisle five!" said the clerk.

(Still a small "s" for said)

✓ "The milk is on aisle five, right?" said the clerk.

Write your speech sentence the same, even if interrupted by action or a dialogue tag

Sometimes you may choose to break up the speech of a character with an action or a dialogue tag. Let's take a look at action first.

CORRECT:

✔ "Marty, come back here!" Mom said. "Your homework isn't done."

Since Mom is saying two separate sentences, there is a period after said.

INCORRECT:

✘ "Marty, come back here!" Mom said, "your homework isn't done."

How do I know this isn't correct?
If I took out the dialogue tag, it would look like this:

✘ "Marty, come back here! your homework isn't done."

See? The word "your" should be capitalized because this is, in fact, two separate sentences. And since the first sentence is complete, there shouldn't be a comma after "Mom said."

What about one long sentence broken up with action or dialogue tags? You would write it this way:

✔ "Okay, the thing is," Angela said, pacing the room, "we need to find the map to the treasure before the pirates do."

Here I've included a dialogue tag (**Angela said**) and an action (**pacing the room**). Because this is one long sentence, the dialogue tag and action are set off by commas and not periods.

When the second part of the sentence picks up again,

"we need to find the map..."

we DON'T capitalize the first letter because this is still the same sentence.

ANOTHER SIDE NOTE

Write the sentence as you typically would. Don't add in extra capitalizations or periods just because you are inserting a dialogue tag or action into the middle of it.

ARE YOU CONFUSED YET?!

Let's take some examples from our three stories and see some of these rules getting broken. See if you can catch the mistakes.

Fairies in the Baseboards

"Come on, Tito! I exclaimed, we have to get past that cat." Tito shivered. "It's too scary. He looked up at the big cat. I don't think we can make it!" "Look, I'll distract him, and you run past into that little hole. Okay?" "I took Tito by the shoulders. I know you can do it!"

Whew! There are a lot of mistakes going on, but most of them really are the same two mistakes happening over and over. Did you spot them?

If you guessed not jumping to a new line with each speaker change and putting quotes around the action sentences, you are right! 50 points to Gryffindor.

Let's fix this mess. This is how I would mark the page if I were correcting this:

Example 1–CORRECTED

"Come on, Tito!" I exclaimed. "We have to get past that cat."

Tito shivered. "It's too scary." He looked up at the big cat. "I don't think we can make it!"

"Look, I'll distract him, and you run past into that little hole. Okay?" I took Tito by the shoulders. "I know you can do it!"

Junie and Roger Get Zapped

“Excuse me, I’m looking for my dog who is lost. Have you seen him”?

“No, I don’t think so. Sorry”.

Roger ran up and smelled the girl.

“You smell awful”!

“They’re always getting into something, right”?

“Yes”.

“Sorry about your dog. I will definitely keep my eye out”.

Okay, that's a hot mess! We have people talking, no idea who they are, and possibly even the dog just said someone smelled bad. Plus, the punctuation is all outside of the quotation marks.

Let's see if we can fix this:

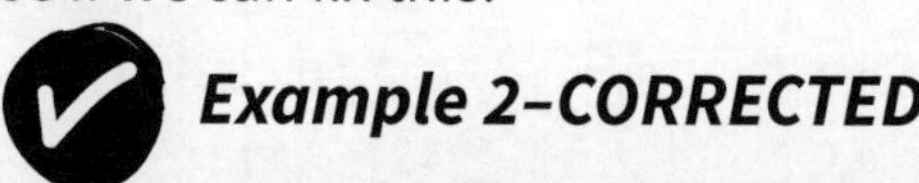

Junie opened the door. A sad girl was standing there.

Adding a detail about the setting gives context to the scene. No talking heads!

"Excuse me, I'm looking for my dog who is lost. Have you seen him?"

Punctuation goes inside the quotation marks.

Add an action tag.

Junie shook her head "No, I don't think so. Sorry."

Punctuation goes inside the quotation marks.

Roger ran up and smelled the girl.

Junie wrinkled her nose and looked down at Roger. "You smell awful!" she said. "They're always

Adding these details shows who's talking and who smells bad.

Punctuation goes inside the quotation marks.

A dialogue tag makes it clear that it's Junie who's speaking.

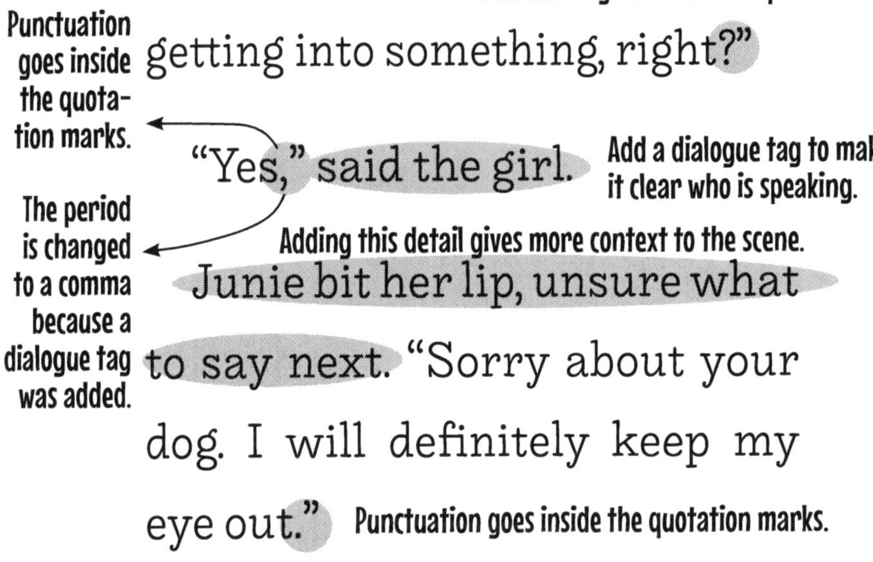

This is much better. Now we know who is saying what. The dog is stinky (not the girl), and the punctuation is all in the proper place within the quotation marks.

Let's look at one final example. This one will be harder, but try your best to spot the mistakes!

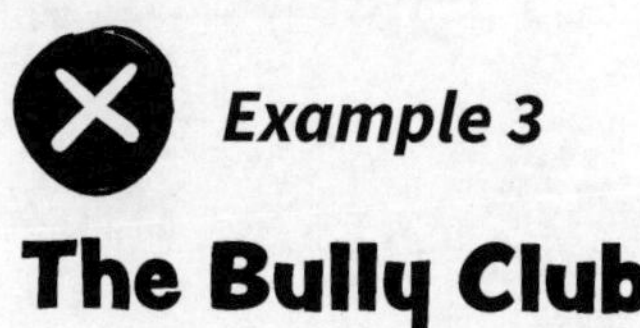

The Bully Club

Oliver quieted everyone down. The first official meeting was under way.

"Thank you for coming." Oliver said, clearing his throat. "I think we can all agree there is a bullying problem at this school."

The crowd murmured in consent.

A small boy spoke up. "Yeah! Last week," he stood up. "They slammed me in my locker. I still have a bruise on my arm!" He raised it for everyone to see."

"Exactly." Said Oliver. "This happens every day to somebody in this room." Oliver surveyed the crowd. At least 35 kids had shown up on the first day alone! He felt hope rising in his chest.

"So, how do we stop it?" Said Brayden, "They're bigger than us."

"Maybe in size, but not in numbers. I have a plan."

Did you find the mistakes? Remember the "Sometimes periods need to be commas rule?" Also, remember how to punctuate when a long sentence is interrupted? These are the two big problems going on in this passage. Let's fix them.

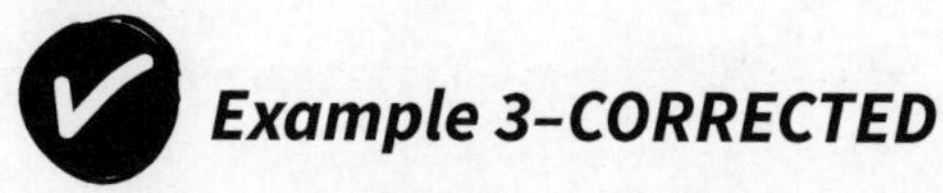

Example 3–CORRECTED

Oliver quieted everyone down. The first official meeting was underway.

Period changed to a comma.

"Thank you for coming," Oliver said, clearing his throat. "I think we can all agree there is a bullying problem at this school."

The crowd murmured in consent.

This sentence isn't finished, so this is a comma instead of a period and the 't' in 'they' is lowercase.

A small boy spoke up. "Yeah! Last week," he stood up, "they slammed me in my locker. I still have a bruise on my arm!" He raised it for everyone to see.

No quotation marks here – this is an action, not speech.

Comma instead of a period, and the 's' in 'said' is lowercase.

"Exactly," said Oliver. "This happens every day to somebody in this room." Oliver surveyed the crowd. At least 35 kids had shown up on the first day alone! He felt hope rising in his chest.

Lowercase

"So, how do we stop it?" said Brayden. "They're bigger than us."

This is a period because Brayden is saying two sentences here, not one.

"Maybe in size, but not in numbers. I have a plan."

Two types of dialogue – Internal and External

Did you know there are two different kinds of dialogue? Well, if you didn't, I'm sure you do now after reading this heading.

External dialogue refers to the usual kind and all of the examples above. This is where characters are talking to other characters *externally*, or outside of themselves.

Internal dialogue refers to speech *inside* of a character. In other words, it is the thoughts the character is thinking that we, the readers, get to hear as well.

Let's look at an example of internal dialogue from *Fairies in the Baseboards*. This scene takes place when the two children of the house find Gabby and Tito and set them up in their dollhouse:

> *The red-haired human, the older sister, set us onto the second floor of the house. It was so high up and decked out with over-sized furniture.*
>
> *"It fits them! They're just like our dolls!" squealed the littler girl.*
>
> *Fits? That's debatable.*
>
> *"Sit down," said the bigger girl.*
>
> *Tito and I peered up at the pink couch made of some kind of shiny hard material. What kind of dolls used a couch this big!*
>
> *I gave Tito a boost onto the tall couch, and then he helped pull me up. The children's faces came close to examine us as we sat there. I have to admit I was struck a little by how monstrous they were! Were they genuinely friendly? What if they were just pretending to be our friends so they could fatten us up? I began to doubt all my theories about humans and wondered if maybe I had just gotten us into a whole heap of trouble?*

Now let's look at the same passage where I have highlighted the internal dialogue in bold:

The red-haired human, the older sister, set us onto the second floor of the house. It was so high up and decked out with over-sized furniture.

"It fits them! They're just like our dolls!" squealed the littler girl.

Fits? That's debatable.

"Sit down," said the bigger girl.

Tito and I peered up at the pink couch made of some kind of shiny hard material. ***What kind of dolls used a couch this big!***

I gave Tito a boost onto the tall couch, and then he helped pull me up. The children's faces came close to examine us as we sat there. I have to admit I was struck a little by how monstrous they were! ***Were they genuinely friendly? What if they were just pretending to be our friends so they could fatten us up?*** *I began to doubt all my theories about humans.* ***What if I had just gotten us into a whole heap of trouble?***

Adding in some internal dialogue can help your readers connect in a personal way to your main character. However, if you overdo it, you may slow down the action of the scene/chapter/book, so be careful! Use it sparingly, but when needed.

HOW TO WRITE DIALOGUE THAT SOUNDS NATURAL

Have you ever read a book, and the way the characters talk just doesn't sound very convincing? When we write words for our characters, we need to pay attention to a couple of things:

Dialogue should be consistent with the character

Knowing your character, would they say something like this? Think about how your character talks, their voice, and try to stay true to that every time they speak.

Dialogue should not be cluttered

Natural Dialogue doesn't, um, include, like, everything people actually say, right? If you listened to your friends talking and wrote every word down, you would hear a LOT of filler words: um, uh, like, so, and then. It's okay to have your character speak like this if they're nervous, or if it's part of their character, but a little bit goes a long way. If you write *too* true to life, your dialogue won't come across as natural. It will come across as cluttered and clunky. Writing good dialogue means trying to sound like real people, but pared down.

Now that you know the tools and rules of crafting great dialogue, we are ready to think about the moment your story has been building toward this whole time—the climax!

STEP 10

BUILD TO THE CLIMAX

Have you ever noticed that the action at the end of a movie gets pretty intense? Everything seems to build and build until the characters find themselves in more and more impossible situations. You begin to wonder how in the world they will ever get out of this.

The moment when everything comes to a head is called the climax. It is the point when the villain has forced the ultimate showdown, or the conflict has built up to a boiling point. The climax is the moment in the story that everything has been moving toward. It will decide the fate of everything. There is no way you want to miss the climax of the movie, no matter how much your bladder is regretting getting that Big Gulp size drink! Nobody wants to miss the climax.

Why?

Because it is the emotional payoff we are craving after following the whole story!

If the climax is good, we feel yes, this is the inevitable and perfect conclusion to everything that has happened up to that moment. It makes sense and feels right.

If the climax is terrible, we throw the book across the room or storm out of the theater complaining to our friends what a lame story that was.

The climax is the do-or-die moment for your whole story!

That can sound pretty scary. But take a breath. You are going to write a good climax.

How do I know?

Because you've put in the work.

A good climax is born out of the action, plot, conflict, characters, and everything you have been developing in your story up until this point. It is just the natural end to all you have established so far.

But there are some qualities that any great climactic moment needs. Here are some key things to keep in mind:

Increase External Conflict

Everything should get bigger, faster, more intense as you move toward the climax. Remember the time bomb trick we learned back in step 8? Is there a way you can shorten the fuse? What if your characters needed to complete all their tasks in a set amount of time, but that time just got cut in half? Brainstorm how you can increase the tension and conflict going on in this last push of your story.

Increase Internal Conflict

Internal conflict is the pulling forces inside your characters. It is their split allegiances. In *The Bully Club*, Oliver is so committed to fighting the bullies he doesn't realize he is becoming a bully himself. When he finally sees it, there is a conflict inside—does he keep his club and his new sense of power, or does he stay true to his belief that bullying is wrong?

Increasing internal conflict is especially important in "quieter" stories, where there are no car chases, moments of mortal peril, etc. Even if your story is about middle school and no one is in danger of losing life and limb, how can you ramp up what is at stake to your character? Play into their deep desires/wants and fears. How can you make what is happening to your characters worse? This is not the time to be nice! Throw everything you can at them, and then help them be victorious anyways. Your readers will love it.

Use Setting/Location to Ramp up Intensity

Will your big showdown between your villain and your hero take place atop a tall building or in an old lady's living room with tea on the coffee table? The choice of where to place your final action can make or break your climax. Use your setting to your advantage for these final climactic scenes. Chances are there is much to gain and much to lose from your climax. How can you *show* that through your setting? Are your characters approaching ever-increasing danger? Describe what that looks like. Try to translate the feelings of your characters and their perception of their environment into the details you tell your reader.

And remember, you have the power to set the stage almost anywhere as long as it makes sense in your story world. Are you making the most of this power? Don't be lazy! Figure out the most thrilling, terrifying, death-defying location to have your climactic scenes take place, and let your setting add to the drama of this most dramatic part of your story. On the other hand, don't force the characters somewhere they wouldn't normally be!

Structure your final chapters and scenes to add to the tension

Remember, the climax is the final release from the tension we have created in this home stretch of the novel. Your pacing should be at a growing speed with unrelenting momentum. This is not the time to include those "catch a breath" scenes or have your characters go to the library for research. This is the time to build and keep the tension high until the end of the climax.

Structure your chapters and scenes to increase the tension—shorter sentences, action, and revelations at every turn, cliff-hangers that keep us involved. Keeping scenes tight and action-packed helps to keep the forward momentum going.

Take a look at this example of a good climax from *Junie and Roger Get Zapped*. Junie has just realized she is hearing a second voice in her head that is not Roger's! They realize it is a squirrel. Roger says he knows how to find the missing dog, Winston, and he knows where the villainous squirrel is, but they have to act fast! Junie's parents call her that it is time to leave for her sister's play, and Junie must decide who to obey. Here is what happens next:

Junie stared at Roger. "You mean the squirrel, the one who got zapped with us, is responsible for Macy's dog disappearing?!"

Roger nodded, and, in her mind, he said, "Yes! I told you, the squirrels are EVIL! We have to go now! I know where he is."

"But the play..."

"Junie!" Mom called from the kitchen. "Stick Roger out so we can go. We're running late!"

Junie bit her lip and looked at Roger.

"Listen to me," Roger said. "We have to find that squirrel!"

Junie knew to miss that play would mean being grounded for life, but she looked at Roger and took a deep breath. "Okay, let's go."

She quickly dashed off a note to her parents, grabbed a shoe box to catch the squirrel in, along with a handful of peanuts, and slipped out the back door with Roger at her side.

They ran all the way to the forest park. She hadn't bothered to leash Roger and was struggling to keep up with him.

"Slow down!" she yelled.

Roger stepped into the tree line and froze. He perked his ears and smelled the ground. "This way," he told Junie.

They ran again until they came to the large oak tree in the center of the park.

"How do you know he'll be here?" Junie asked, out of breath.

"The squirrel mentioned the giant oak in his thoughts," said Roger. "He's meeting his girlfriend here at dusk."

Junie looked past the trees at the sun sinking behind the horizon.

"Move fast, put the nuts in the box," Roger instructed.

With the trap set, the two hid behind a neighboring tree. Junie was just starting to doubt that the squirrel would show when she heard chattering in the branches overhead.

Roger stared at her. "It's him." Then he focused all his energy on the box. His small muscular legs were quivering.

And then it happened! The squirrel came to the base of the tree and froze. He smelled the breeze. Junie held her breath. Had the squirrel spotted them? Smelled them? He didn't seem to. He turned toward the trap and peered into the box. Junie focused in on him. She could just make out his tiny voice.

"Peanuts! A treasure! Hoomans so dumb, leave treasures."

Then he laughed a high-pitched maniacal laugh and dove into the box.

No sooner had he jumped in before Roger crashed out of his hiding spot and flipped the box over with the squirrel inside! Junie, running up behind, pinned the box to the ground.

The box exploded with angry squeaks and scratching and scampering, but Junie held fast.

"Tricksy Hoomans and puppers!" the squirrel yelled. And then he broke out in a string of indistinguishable words that Junie guessed were rodent curse words.

Roger barked short excited barks and bounced around. "We got him, we got him!" he exclaimed to Junie's mind.

Junie quieted her mind and focused on the squirrel. She tried to send him a message. "We won't hurt you, but we need to know where the curly dog is. We think you led him on a chase to get lost."

She heard the tiny voice come, fuzzy at first, then clearer.

"I tell you nothing, Hooman!"

Junie, keeping the box pinned to the ground, looked at Roger. "What now?" she thought.

Roger stopped his bouncing and growled. "Now we eat him!" he said in an angry voice.

Junie was startled. That didn't sound like Roger. "No!" she cried. Then she saw Roger give her the slightest wink. He was tricking him! She guarded her thoughts, though, so the squirrel wouldn't hear and continued to play along. "I won't let you!"

"Then I'll bite you!" Roger growled and crept closer and closer.

The squirrel's resolve broke. "No! No! Please, Hooman, don't let puppers eats me! I tell you, I tell you!"

Junie leaned over the box. "Then do it!" she ordered.

The squirrel's confession came. "I lead curly puppers three moons ago. Make him crazy, round and round, to get lost. He not know way out, he go other way, to other street."

"And then what?" Junie focused her thoughts on him, feeling disappointment rising. Three days ago? Macy's dog could be anywhere by now!

"I not know," the squirrel sobbed. "I not know!"

Junie felt sorry for him.

Roger nodded at her, and she lifted the box. The brown squirrel looked at them with squinting eyes, as if stepping out of years of solitary confinement in a dark, damp jail. Then he registered his freedom and zipped up the tree.

"I get you for this!" screeched the squirrel, chattering and shaking his tail. "I get you!" And then he was gone.

Junie fell into the tree in a heap of despair. "We still *don't know where the dog is, and now I'm in major trouble!"*

Did you notice any tricks I used to keep the action going and the tension high in this climactic end to the story? Look how the stakes were raised by Junie having to be in two places at the same time. The dilemma forced her to have internal conflict about which choice to make. Also, look how there was a time bomb placed in the scene. Not only does she have a tough choice to make, but she has very little time to act and decide—if she doesn't move now, they will lose the squirrel, but she also needs to go to the play with her family.

Did you also see the way there is a lot of dialogue and action in these scenes? And there are moments when we begin to wonder if our heroes will be successful at all—introducing these new setbacks and moments of conflict help to increase the excitement.

So, what would a bad climactic scene look like for this story? What if we just gave Junie all the time in the world, nowhere to be, no internal conflict. And then Roger said that he felt like going on a walk. What if they also went to the pet store, bought him a new rubber pork chop, and then Junie ran into her friend, and they talked a bunch about school. Then Roger and Junie end up at the park and see the squirrel who waltzes over and admits what happened to the dog (no conflict, he has nothing to lose).

That would be pretty lame, wouldn't it!? So much meandering and so many useless scenes that slow the pacing down. Zero drama or conflict. I say we stick with the better version.

Now that you've learned all about the climax of the story, you're done, right?

Not so fast.

What if we just ended the whole book here? After all, we had our climactic battle with the villain, right? What more is there to do?

Well, actually, a lot more.

We need to *end* this story. We need a resolution.

STEP 11

RESOLVE YOUR STORY

Now it is time to talk about resolution. Why is resolution important? Because you can't just have someone hanging off the edge of a cliff, pull them back over and run the end credits, right?

That would be crazy!

We need to see the characters make it back to some relative normal, even if it's a new normal. Because of their adventures, they will have obviously changed, but the story's resolution gives us a chance to see that—to see the changed characters in their life now. For a story to feel complete, we usually need to come full circle back to where we began. This is what the resolution part of your story should be all about.

In *The Wizard of Oz*, the climax happens when Dorothy throws water on the wicked witch and defeats her once and for all. However, if the story just ended there, it wouldn't feel right. What about getting back to Kansas? What about "There's no place like home?"

This is where resolution comes in. We need to *resolve* some things so that the reader can get to "The End" with a sense of satisfaction.

So, how do you do that?

Here are five ways to create a satisfying resolution:

A resolution should resolve

Don't leave Dorothy in Oz or Harry Potter standing with his wand after just defeating Voldemort. Don't leave your readers saying, "Now what?" The resolution section of the story is where you tie all the loose ends up. Well, at least the major and important ones. Have you given a satisfying ending to your primary plotline and minor subplots? Have you created a scene to show your characters back in their normal world, or their world's "new normal" from their changed perspective? These are all significant details to include.

A resolution shouldn't be too short

We don't want Dorothy to kill the witch and then say a quick see-ya to her friends and run off. That would leave the audience/readers feeling a bit of whiplash. Give enough time to slow the pace down from the hectic go, go, go of the scenes leading up to, and including, the climax. One or two lines, even one paragraph, is not enough for a resolution. In a short story, yes. In a novel, no. Make sure you give your readers adequate time to catch their breath and settle in for this final scene or chapter.

A resolution shouldn't be too long

While we need the resolution to be long enough to establish a sense of normal, we also need to know when enough is enough. You don't want to drag it out so your readers wonder why the story hasn't ended yet! Finding this sweet spot, the right ending place, will come with practice. What if Dorothy made it back to Oz, woke up and saw her family and friends, and then got out of bed, made some biscuits, took a bath, and started helping Auntie Em with her quilt project. We might be wondering what the point of all these scenes is! Don't do that. Get in, resolve the story and loose ends, and get out.

Create an excellent ending image

By the end of your novel, your readers will come to feel a connection with your characters. Think about it! They've followed them through thick and thin, been with them through down times and good times. They know their fears, their hopes, their accomplishments. Hopefully, they have come to know and love them as you do. That being said, don't just take your characters and jump on the quickest train out of town! Give your readers a chance to slow down and say goodbye. Think about the last feeling you want to leave them with. In the *Star Wars* movies, this final scene is often a group moment, with the whole gang together. They are happy, excited for all they've accomplished, and connected to one another. It makes us feel good too. Who wouldn't want to hug a Wookie? I know I would.

Don't rush it

This is not the time to rush. You're so close to finishing your novel, and I know you can't wait to type those last lines. The temptation will be strong, but you must resist! As stated above, this is the ending of everything you've worked so hard for. Don't sell it short and rush through it because you are just ready to be done. Or, if you can't resist that, make sure you come back to the ending and work on it when you're refreshed. Try writing a couple of different endings and get feedback on which seems to be the best.

Let's look at what the Resolution sections of the book would look like for one of our sample stories, *Fairies in the Baseboards*. Since we are focusing on the Resolution and end, our synopsis will start with the last part of Act 2 and go through the end of the book. This happens right after the two fairies, Gabby and Tito, are discovered by the kids of the house, two sisters who are ages five and seven:

The kids are delighted and set the fairies up in their doll house. At first, it's amazing. Gabby feels like a queen in such a big house! But she's is disappointed when the kids seem to think the fairies are toys to be played with. She begins to think maybe she misjudged the Humans when one of the girls hurts Tito's arm with her roughhousing. Maybe they are just big monsters like everyone in her world says. She and Tito fly down from the dollhouse and hide in a hole in the baseboards.

But Gabby is surprised when the girls are sad about Tito's arm and losing their new friends. They realize their behavior caused his injury and start to understand the fairies are real, living beings who deserve respect. The girls ask the fairies to forgive them and ask for another chance. Gabby chooses to forgive the girls, and Tito reluctantly agrees to give the Humans another chance.

The fairies and girls stay up late, telling stories and learning about each other's worlds. Gabby watches the girls as they fall asleep and thinks about how it isn't that different from the countless times she's watched her little sister sleeping. Tito snores, but Gabby feels so many things she can't stop thinking. While the girls are big and different from fairies, Gabby can tell inside them is even bigger. She realizes there is much to learn and discover about humans, and there are good ones and bad ones. Which, she thinks, is not that different from fairies.

Gabby is awakened, sleeping on the girl's bed, to a rescue team (kind of like a SWAT team). She and Tito are taken back to their world, and everyone wants to know how they survived interacting with the Humans (who have such big teeth). Did the Humans try to eat them? How did they manage to be so brave? Tito loves to tell all the stories, but Gabby just wants to go home.

Back at home, she starts in on her homework. She opens the book, and the chapter is "Avoiding Being Eaten By Humans." She shuts the book and instead makes a tent with her sheet and lights it up inside. She opens a new notebook and writes, "The True Story of Humans. Chapter One - Humans are not Monsters."

Did you notice where the plot points were—the Dark Moment, the Turning Point, the Climax, the Resolution? Let's look at the passage again, with the plot points highlighted:

The kids are delighted and set the fairies up in their doll house. At first, it is amazing. Gabby feels like a queen in such a big house! **[Beginning of Dark Moment]** But she's is disappointed when the kids seem to think the fairies are toys to be played with. She begins to think maybe she misjudged the Humans when one of the girls hurts Tito's arm with her roughhousing. Maybe they are just big monsters like everyone in her world says. She and Tito fly down from the dollhouse and hide in a hole in the baseboards. **[End of Dark Moment]**

[Beginning of Turning Point] But Gabby is surprised when the girls are sad for Tito and the loss of their new friends. They realize their behavior caused his injury and start to understand the fairies are real, living beings who deserve respect. The girls ask the fairies to forgive them and ask for another chance. Gabby chooses to forgive the girls, and Tito reluctantly agrees to give the Humans another chance. **[End of Turning Point]**

[Beginning of Climax] The fairies and girls stay up late, telling stories and learning about each other's worlds. Gabby watches the girls as they fall asleep and thinks about how it isn't that different from the countless times she's watched her little sister sleeping. Tito snores, but Gabby feels so many things she can't stop thinking. While the girls are big and different from fairies, Gabby can tell inside them is even bigger. She realizes there is much to learn and discover about humans, and there are good ones and bad ones. Which, she thinks, is not that different from fairies. **[End of Climax]**

[Beginning of Resolution] Gabby is awakened, sleeping on the girl's bed, to a rescue team (kind of like a SWAT team). She and Tito are taken back to their world, and everyone wants to know how they survived interacting with the Humans (who have such big teeth). Did the Humans try to eat them? How did they manage to be so brave? While holding his arm in a sling, Tito loves to tell all the stories, but Gabby wants to go home.

Back at home, she starts in on her homework. She opens the book, and the chapter is "Avoiding Being Eaten By Humans." She shuts the book and instead makes a tent with her sheet and lights it up inside. She opens a new notebook and writes, "The True Story of Humans. Chapter One - Humans are not Monsters." **[End of Resolution]**

This is a "quieter" story, so the climax is not full of car chases and death-defying stakes. But it is still the moment where the story's goal, to find out how humans really are, is accomplished. This is what Gabby has been trying to do for the whole story.

For the resolution, did you see how Gabby took what she learned from her story journey and how it changed her? She is now ready to stand up to the false ideas she was scared to challenge before.

Did you also notice how we didn't show Gabby writing her *whole* book, or the reception it received from her teachers and friends? We don't need all of that. This is the right place to end this story. It is almost as if this story is ending right on the brink of a new one! That is a great place to stop. And also, a great chance to write a sequel.

Congratulations! If you get to this point in your story, you have reached "The End," and that is amazing!

Now you probably think it is time to load that puppy onto Amazon and self-publish it or ship it off to a publisher, right?

Wrong!

There is one final task on the road to completing your novel, and it can be a path laid with mines, thorny vines, and beasts waiting in the shadows. But you can't avoid it! You must travel through it.

It is the path of revising and editing your book.

But don't worry—I'm here to walk you through it each step of the way.

So, let's go!

STEP 12

REVISE AND EDIT

It can't be said enough that completing a novel, and your first novel, is no small task! How many people start and never get past the first few chapters? Or, how many get lost in the middle and never find their way out? By reaching the end of your novel, you have joined a small group of writers. Congratulations! Soak all that sense of accomplishment in and remember these good feelings.

Now, as we said earlier, you may be tempted to take your novel and send it out into the world. Don't do that! At least, not yet.

What is the number one complaint literary agents and publishers have about the books they get sent? They aren't revised!

A book that is not revised is a first draft. A first draft may be pretty good, especially if you have taken the time in the beginning to plot it out well and really think about your story. If you've done this front-end work, congratulations! That means the work of revision will be that much easier for you. However, it doesn't give you a "Get out of Revision Free" card.

Your story, your beautiful story that you have poured yourself into, still needs work. You may feel this realization as highly disappointing and think, "What do you mean?! I'm done!" You are done with telling the story, or at least the first version of it, but you are not done with it yet.

For instance, pretend you are a gardener and grow a shrub that you will one day shape into one of those topiaries—you know, the bushes that look like a rabbit or a bear. While your bush is growing is not the time to start whacking off branches. Or, maybe it is (I don't make topiaries). But the point is, this is the time you are writing your first draft. You can shape it to a point, but you have to let it grow. You have to let your ideas and your story come out and fill up the space. If you start hacking away at something still growing, you might cut too much, and it will die. Your first draft was the time you were letting your tiny story idea grow and mature.

But now, when you are ready to begin revising and creating your second draft, this is the time to stand back and look at what you have grown. Now is the time to take the pruning shears, and sometimes the chainsaw, and look for the shape the story wants to be. There will be parts that are sticking out and don't help anything. Snip. There will be sections that are too dense and take away from the shape of what you want to create. Cut those out. Now that you have something to work with, you can see your story in its totality—what is missing, what is overdone, what works, and what doesn't.

Revising is hard. It can almost feel as hard as writing the story, to begin with. If you love a section of your book, but you realize it just doesn't work or is a distraction from your story, cutting it out can feel like digging out a piece of your heart with an ice cream scoop. You might think, "I can't cut Bernie the clown! I love him." But if Bernie doesn't serve a real purpose in your book, he needs to go. It stinks, but it's the truth. Plus, lots of people don't like clowns.

So, how do you navigate the path of revising your story? Here are four Revision pitfalls to avoid:

Don't get discouraged

You are bound to feel a little saddened when you realize the book you just spent all this time on isn't as good as you hoped it would be and still know it can be. This is totally normal! Let the feelings come, grab some tissues, eat some ice cream, then set all that aside. Do you know who else's first draft wasn't as good as they hoped?

Um, only EVERY WRITER WHO EVER LIVED!

Seriously!

Shakespeare? He revised.

J.K. Rowling? Also, a reviser.

Dave Pilkey? Yep. Aaron Blabey? Yep. Yep.

Every other author you love? You guessed it!

Revision is necessary, but just because your book isn't perfect from the get-go doesn't mean it's garbage. It means you're following the process for writing a novel. Don't give up on it!

Make "good" even better

Once you've accepted that your first draft needs to be revised, remember to look for ways to make what is already good, better, and what is terrible, disappear. Cutting is your friend. Weird subplots that don't tie in, unnecessary characters, dialogue that goes too long and is pointless, descriptions that stretch on forever—all of these are prime examples of what to cut. There might be other areas in which you need to add more information, such as developing what your characters are feeling or reacting.

Start with significant changes and work toward smaller ones

You can spend twenty minutes making sure each word and sentence is beautifully written in a paragraph, but what if you end up cutting that whole scene later? What if you edit and edit a scene so it's finally great, and then you cut the entire chapter? See what I mean! You will avoid wasting time editing things that will be cut anyway if you make the significant changes first and then work with what you have left.

But, how do you make big changes or cuts? If you haven't plotted your book yet, do it now! Try to see how your plot unfolds. This is called doing a structural or developmental edit. Basically, make sure the Acts have the right proportions to each other and that you don't have 37 chapters in Act 1, five in Act 2, and seven in Act 3. Figuring out your plot structure allows you to see what doesn't fit, what needs to be moved, and much more. If you already created a plot in the beginning, break it out now. How did your actual book deviate from your original story?

A lot of times, the way we go off our outline ends up being great. Sometimes it doesn't. Just create or change your plot structure to fit the book you want to write. This should help you see where you have plot holes, need to add more, or where you need to cut chapters or scenes. You may even find you need a whole new opening to better set up the book for where your story is headed (this is common), or you may need to re-write your ending.

After you are pretty happy with the structure of your story, you can dive down into individual chapters and see if each part of the chapter is necessary to the story. If something isn't necessary either to the plot, character development, or because it adds a lot of fun to your book, it very likely should be cut. This is what the second draft is all about—big picture revisions.

The third draft: going from "better" to great

Now you are ready to begin your third draft. Your big picture structure is pretty good. You've cut a lot of extra fluff and distracting parts. What do you do now? Now get into each chapter, each scene, each paragraph, each sentence. Cut out filler words, such as that, really, seemed, very, kind of. There are many more—just Google "filler words in writing" and you will get a good-sized list!

Cut out some of your descriptions. Pick your best image of what the woods were like, and use that.

Check your verbs and make sure you use active verbs that are precise to the action you describe.

Read your book out loud or listen to it played to you through a text-to-speech program. Both Microsoft Word and Google Docs have text-to-speech capabilities. The computer will read back what you wrote. Hearing your words out loud is very helpful for catching minor mistakes, typos, and clunky sentences.

Read your book and note the places you were bored. Look for ways to cut those sections or shorten them.

Make sure your dialogue formatting is correct and flows well. Again, there is no replacement for listening to it out loud. Does it sound like actual speech? If not, re-work it.

When you have done all this, and of course, ran it through spell check, you are ready to move to an exciting part of the editing process—Beta readers!

BETA READERS

What are Beta readers? Beta readers are people who are the first audience for your book. They can be people you know and trust, such as family and friends, but they can also be people you don't know very much. I suggest starting with people you know, and preferably people who are similar to your ideal audience. For example, if your story is an epic fantasy about vampires in the Wild West, don't have your grandma read it when she hates monsters and cowboys. Ask your best friend who also likes the kinds of books you do!

Letting other people finally see your book can be both exciting and nerve-wracking! It is scary to show your work and hear someone's honest feedback. However, whatever opinions you get, it is important to remember two things:

There are people who love and hate every book out there

Even a great book has people who hate it. Even classic books and *New York Times* Best-sellers. Your goal is not to write a book everyone will love. Your goal is to write a book people who like what you like will love. So, again, you are not writing for your vampire-hating Nana.

Other people can see problems that you can't

This is hard to learn, but it is true! Why do we need other people to look at our work and tell us what they think? Because we aren't able to see our work clearly. If you wrote a scene with roller-skating poodles, you might think you explained why this is plausible because *you* know that the poodles spent the first five years of their life in the circus. But remember that chapter you cut because it slowed things down? That was the circus backstory chapter. Your readers will come along and get to the roller-skating poodles and be totally confused!

This is one silly example, but basically, you know your story too well to see it clearly and objectively. You also care about it too much and may not be willing to cut something that needs to be cut. Remember Bernie the clown? Beta readers help you see the things you can't see. They will tell you where the story felt slow or boring. They will let you know what was confusing or seemed to come out of nowhere. They are an invaluable part of the revision process.

It can be hard to hear criticism of your work. Sometimes you might feel angry or hurt. The best thing to do is calm down, set the criticism aside (maybe write the comments down), and then don't think about it for a few days. When you are feeling less touchy, get it out and see if it has any merit. One way to know is if other people have also made the same comments. Another is if you trust the person who is telling you this.

Remember, it is hard to tell a friend what you think if you know it might make them upset. Your friend probably felt terrible telling you what they thought, but they did it because they also want your book to be the best it can be. Consider their comments. Your book will be better off for it. And remember, readers or publishers won't know you at all. They only care if the story is good. They won't give it a second chance if it is full of mistakes and underdeveloped sections that your friends tried to warn you about, but you didn't want to listen.

The only exception to this is if your Beta reader is just someone mean, jealous, or there's another issue between you and them. In this case, don't ask that person to read your stuff ever again! And you can probably just ignore most of what they said, as long as nobody else said the same thing.

Now that you have the tools to revise your novel, what is the next step?

If you just want to write a novel and don't care about "putting it out there" you can be done. Now start the next one!

If you want to explore the world of publishing, read on. There is a lot to know. But you can do it!

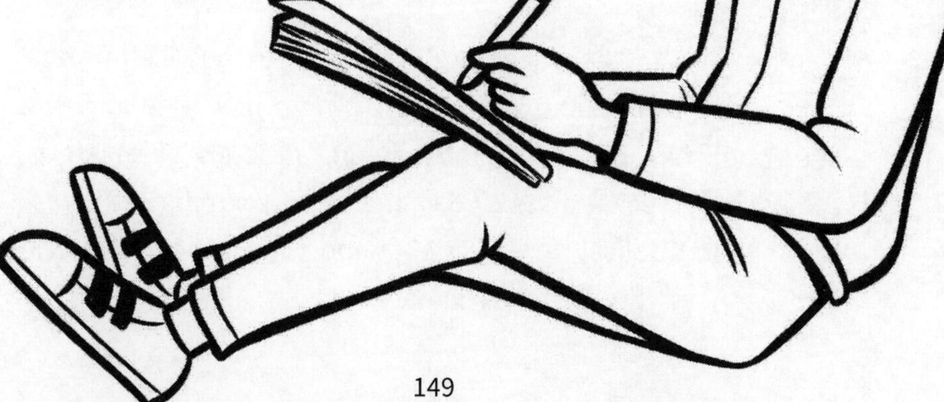

STEP 13

PUBLISH YOUR BOOK

Welcome to the adventure! The path to publication has never been as rich and varied as it is right now. People have been publishing books for almost as long as books (or tablets or scrolls) have been around. Today, there are two main paths you can take to publication: Traditional and Self-publication. Let's explore them both, in no particular order.

Option #1
Traditional Publishing

Traditional publishing is what most of us think of when we think of getting a book published. The bulk of the books at your library are traditionally published, as are the books at your school. Traditional publishers are choosy and agree to publish only a very small number of books that come through their doors. Why is that? Are they just mean?

They are not mean, but they're businesses with a mission to publish books they believe are of high quality, and that will make them money. They want to see great stories that are well-told, unique, and fresh. They want to find the next big author and the next big book. They take their job as publishers seriously.

Traditional publishers will never ask you for money.

The bottom line is, they put a lot of money, time, and resources into the books they choose to publish. This is the main reason they are so particular about which books they publish. They never, ever, EVER ask you to pay them money! This is very important. If a "publisher" ever asks you to pay them money to publish your book, they are not a legitimate publisher, and you should run away, preferably screaming while you run to warn other authors as well.

For the most part, publishers are not open to submissions straight from writers. This is especially true for the big publishers in New York that publish the books you know and love, like *Harry Potter* and *The Diary of a Wimpy Kid*.

You may be wondering, "How do I ever get published then, if I can't send them my book?" This is a good question. You may or may not have heard about Literary Agents, but they are the secret gatekeepers to the publishing world. What is their job? Well, lots of things. But mainly, they accept submissions from writers who want to get their books published. If the agent thinks your story is well-developed and has a unique enough idea, and if it is the kind of story they represent, they may choose to take you on as a client. For you as a writer, this is called "finding representation."

But, pause a minute. What did I mean by saying "if it is the kind of story they represent?" This means that not all agents take on the same kinds of stories or represent the same kinds of authors. It is imperative to do your homework first if you want to go this route. Please don't send a horror story to a Literary Agent who only represents picture books. See what I mean? This just makes them mad.

So, let's say you've researched and found four or five agents you want to query. Now what? And what in the world is "query?" Querying is the process of sending a one-page introductory letter to an agent with a fun pitch for your book, a sentence or two about yourself, and a brief comment about why you think *this* book is a right fit for *them*. It should also include the word count of your project and what genre it falls into. All this can sound confusing, but the web is full of excellent advice on how to write a query letter (also known as a cover letter).

If one of the agents likes your query letter, they may ask you to send them your first ten pages, or maybe the first 50 pages if they like it a lot. If they really like it, they might ask you to send them the entire manuscript. If they do this, you have my permission to dance with excitement!

Now, let's say they call you and decide to be your agent. This is a great day! It is hard to get a legitimate agent. What if you find an agent very easily, let's say they even find you? Then they tell you that it is standard to pay a "reading fee" to read your manuscript or charge you something to represent you. This is a big red flag! Just like with legitimate publishers, legitimate agents don't charge authors anything upfront to represent them. So, if they don't charge you, how do they get paid? Real agents get paid by selling your book to publishers. They will receive a percentage of the money you get from the publisher for your book.

Just like real publishers, agents will never ask you to pay them.

So, what is an agent's job? Their job is to represent you and your book. They'll help you find a publisher who will be the right fit for you and who will purchase your book for publication. They also help edit the book and guide you to get your book as good as possible before sending it out to publishers. Once you have a potential sale of your book, your agent can help you know if it is a good deal or not. They become your business partner in the world of publishing, and that can be very helpful to have!

Can you be traditionally published without an agent? Yes. There are still smaller presses (publishers) that are open to direct submission. The important thing is, no matter if you are submitting to an agent or directly to a publisher, FOLLOW THE SUBMISSION GUIDELINES EXACTLY! Yes, even if it says what font size to use and you think a rule is silly.

This is your first test to see how serious you are and if you can follow directions. You spent so much time writing, revising, and preparing your book for submission. Do you want to blow it all now because you didn't want to take the time to follow the guidelines? They get tons of submissions every day and don't have time to mess with people who can't follow simple instructions or think they are too special that the rules don't apply to them.

Is it hard to be traditionally published? I would be lying if I said it was easy. But it is important to remember that publishers and agents *need* stories to publish. Otherwise, they don't have a business! Do yourself a favor by revising your book, making it the very best it can be, before sending it to an agent. You may get a lot of rejections. But you also might get some excellent advice for what you can do to make your book better. Plus, with every book you write, you will get better yourself. Steve Martin, comedian, actor, and writer, says, "Be so good they can't ignore you." Is this easy? No! But is it rewarding and amazing to put work into your art and feel yourself getting better all the time? Yes!

Option # 2
Self-publishing

Not that long ago, if someone heard the term "self-published," they would assume your book wasn't good enough to be traditionally published. That is not the case today at all! Self-publishing, or sometimes called "Indie" or Independent Publishing, is a legitimate way to become a published author. Many self-published authors have more sales and readers than some traditionally published authors.

So, is this the right option for you? There are several great things about self-publishing.

First, you don't have to have anyone "approve of" your work to get it published. Anyone can self-publish a book. And now, with the revolution of print on demand, it doesn't even have to cost money upfront to buy hundreds of books like it used to. With print-on-demand publishers, such as Amazon or IngramSpark, all you need to do is upload your book to their website and make it available to the public. Anytime someone wants to buy your book, a physical book will be printed and shipped to that person. You get a percentage of the money from that sale. There are also opportunities to publish your book as an electronic book (Ebook).

No one needs to approve your self-published book—which can be both good and bad.

Second, traditional publishers move at a molasses' pace (that means super slow). What if you wrote a book and you don't want to wait two years or more to see it published? Self-publishing may be a good path for you!

Third, you have total control over your book. No one is editing your book before it is published or suggesting you change this or that. No one is picking a cover for you, deciding where your book will be sold, or when it will be released, etc.

Fourth, a lot of traditional publishing is based on "the market." What does this mean? It means publishers are always thinking about what will sell, what the trends are, what might be the next trend. Your book may be beautifully written and the best fantasy book about hedgehogs around, but they'll pass if the publisher doesn't think there is a market for a hedgehog book.

This can be a hard lesson to learn about the publishing industry. But with self-publishing, your beautiful hedgehog book can bypass all this. Maybe they're wrong! Maybe your book *finds* the hedgehog story lovers out there that no one knew existed! This is the exciting thing about self-publishing. With fewer gatekeepers, more unusual and unique stories have their chance to shine.

All these reasons to self-publish may sound too good to be true! No querying process, no trying to sell your book, and hoping for a sale. Why would anyone NOT choose this path?!

Well, there are a few reasons. Remember above when I said no one was editing your book or making a cover for you? Those are all services a traditional publishing house does for you and your book *free of charge*. This is kind of a big deal. If you self-publish, YOU are the editor, proofreader, cover designer, marketing expert, and more! You have to plan the best time for your book to come out; you have to format your text to look good when printed. You have to hire an illustrator yourself if you have pictures. It actually can cost a lot of money and take a lot of time to self-publish a book. Suppose your goal is to make money with your book and become a career author self-publishing. In that case, you need to invest in hiring editors, proofreaders, cover designers, and other professionals to help you get your book off to a great start. You will have to market your book and make sure people know about it!

Still, even with the downsides, self-publishing is an accessible option that has helped many people achieve their dream of being a published author.

Whatever path you choose to publish, or if you don't decide to publish your first book at all, the important thing is you find the path that is right for you and your goals for your book.

YOUNG AUTHORS
These next few pages showcase six well-known authors. Some published their books right away, others waited a few years after their books were finished, but they all have one thing in common—they're all kids! They all wrote their first books while they were still in school, and you can too. Read through their bios and you'll see they're not that different from you.

ALEC GREVEN

Alec wrote and published his first book at just 9 years old! What started as a school project became his book, *How to Talk to Girls*. Apparently, Alec noticed boys on the playground trying to talk to girls and making a lot of mistakes!

His book became a *New York Times* Best-selling book. He has made television appearances on several shows, including *The Tonight Show*. I guess it was so unusual for a 9-year-old to write a book about dating advice that everyone took notice!

Alec has gone on to write four other books: *How to Talk to Moms*, *How to Talk to Dads*, *How to Talk to Santa*, and *Rules for School*.

HOW TO TALK TO GIRLS
HOW TO TALK TO MOMS
HOW TO TALK TO DADS
HOW TO TALK TO SANTA
RULES FOR SCHOOL

11 years old

SURESH & JYOTI GUPTARA

Do you work well with your brother or sister, or do you fight like cats and dogs? These twins, the Guptara brothers, wrote a book together. In fact, they wrote a whole series of books!

They finished the first draft of their fantasy book at just 11 years old. Their book *Conspiracy of Calaspia* was published after many revisions and rewrites when they were 17 years old.

Today as adults, the Guptara twins are not just best-selling authors, they are also journalists and speakers at many literary conventions. According to the twins, their passions include "defending civilization against forces of darkness, and football."

CONSPIRACY
OF CALASPIA

S. E. HINTON

Susan Eloise Hinton started writing her first book at just 15! As a lover of reading, Hinton was frustrated by the Young Adult books available at the time. So, what did she do? She wrote the kind of book she wished was out there. Growing up in Tulsa, OK, Hinton was inspired by a real-life clash where a kid in her high school was beaten up by rich kids. Her book *The Outsiders*, which was published in 1967, is very different from the usual teen books of her time. The story tells about Ponyboy and his friends, "Greasers," who are on the outside of society (they don't have money or popularity). Their enemies are the "Socs" (short for Socials). The book won her many awards and is well-known reading for high school kids even today.

The Outsiders took some time to really take off, but when it did it gave Hinton a lot of attention and fame. Some even called her "The Voice of the Youth." Over her career so far, she has published nine books (four have even been made into movies!).

THE OUTSIDERS

12 years old

GORDON KORMAN

Few young authors have been as prolific as Gordan Korman. Korman wrote his first book while in the 7th grade! According to him, his school must have been short an English teacher that year and put the track and field coach in charge of his English class. Having been given freedom to work on what creative writing he wanted to, Korman started to write a book. With an hour a day to work on it, he completed his book, *This Can't Be Happening at Macdonald Hall*, in four months.

Korman, who was given the job of collecting the Scholastic book orders, decided to send his book in to them to be published (after getting his mom to type it for him). It worked, and the book was published when Korman was just entering high school. Scholastic must have recognized his talent, because today Korman has written more than 90 books for kids and teens!

THIS CAN'T BE HAPPENING AT MACDONALD HALL

12 years old

JAKE MARCIONETTE

Imagine if every holiday and summer break that you had to write at breakfast and lunch because your mom said you had to write a book! That is exactly how things started for Jake Marcionette. What started as something he dreaded eventually became something he enjoyed.

Jake didn't like a lot of the books out there, except for *Diary of a Wimpy Kid*, of course. He wanted to write a book for kids, about kids, by a kid. So, he took notes at school and wrote down the funny things that happened. Then he let his imagination go to town!

He wrote *Just Jake*, about a fictional character named Jake whose life is thrown in a whirlwind when he has to move from Florida to Maryland because of his dad's job.

When his book was done, Jake printed a bunch of copies and had kids read them (this is what we call Beta readers). The kids let him know what they liked and what they didn't. With this insight, Jake revised his book.

Jake has now published three books in the same series, and he homeschools with a virtual school to make time for his busy schedule writing and doing author visits. Jake wants every kid to know that, "I'm no different than any other kid. I just had a dream and went for it."

JUST JAKE

15 years old

CHRISTOPHER PAOLINI

As a homeschooled student, Paolini read a lot and loved going to his local library. As a lover of fantasy and magic, Paolini's daydreams turned into an idea for the novel *Eragon*, which he wrote at the age of 15. He wanted to write a novel that he would enjoy reading and he also wanted to write accurately about the crafts and experiences he depicted in his books. This led to him forging swords, creating chainmail, bows and arrows; felling trees, and even camping out in the wild places of his native Montana.

Paolini spent a year revising the book, then with the help of his parents, he decided to self-publish it. They spent another year getting it ready with copy editing, marketing, designing a cover, and much more. He and his family spent the next two years promoting the book. Then, fortuitously, children's author Carl Hiaasen's son read the book while on vacation in Montana! Hiassen brought the book to his publisher and they decided to publish it!

Eragon was traditionally published in 2003 and was a big hit, even making the *New York Times* Best-Seller list and becoming a movie. Paolini went on to publish three other books in the series and has inspired many young writers around the world to write their own stories.

SO, WHAT IS THE BOOK YOU WISH YOU COULD READ? WHAT STORY IS AROUND YOU THAT NO ONE IS TELLING? GO AHEAD AND WRITE IT!

13 STEPS WORKSHEETS

The worksheets on the following pages will help you take action and put pen to paper. Follow the steps and write your first novel before you turn 13!

If you need more space that what's provided, you can always photocopy the sheets or use blank paper. When you start the process of writing, you'll need your own paper or computer, but use the worksheets to refer to as you write.

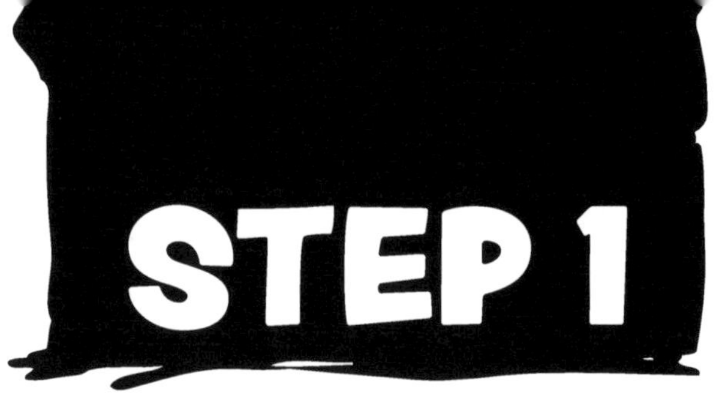

STEP 1

LISTEN TO YOUR CREATIVE IDEAS

Listen to your creative ideas.
Create the space you need to listen to your imagination and find your story.

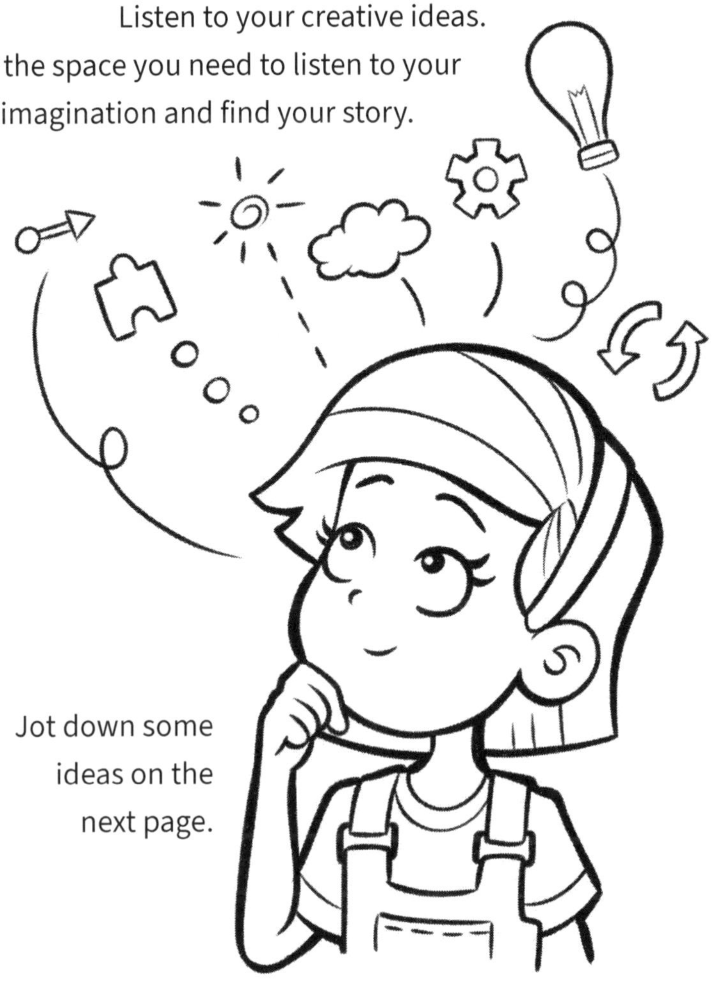

Jot down some ideas on the next page.

IDEAS

BUILD YOUR FOUNDATION

Story-making is really just imagining *what* happens and coming up for believable reasons *why* it happens.

Use the next page to write a synopsis of your story idea. Don't worry—you can always change it later!

CREATE PROFILES FOR ALL YOUR CHARACTERS

Get to know who's starring in your story!
Fill out the Character Questionnaire for your main character, your villain (if you have one), and two other characters. You can photocopy these pages or write down your answers on a separate piece of paper for each character.

IMPORTANT! This information you've filled out on these pages is for you alone. Most of it, if not all, will never appear in your novel! The only character details that need to show up in your story are the relevant ones. I can't stress this enough! Many stories are weighed down by unnecessary information, such as a character got braces in the fourth grade and their favorite animal is the elephant. Unless there's a reason to bring up these details, your readers DON'T NEED TO KNOW THIS.

This exercise is for you so that you can envision your character as accurately as possible. If you see them clearly, you'll write them in a way that we can see them. But please, please, don't tell us about their hatred of Brussels sprouts unless it's essential to your story. Okay? Good.

YOUR CHARACTER'S NAME

AGE

DESCRIBE YOUR CHARACTER IN ONE OR TWO SENTENCES

HOW/WHEN WILL THIS CHARACTER BE INTRODUCED INTO YOUR STORY?

APPEARANCE

WHAT DOES YOUR CHARACTER LOOK LIKE?

ANY SPECIAL FEATURES (A SCAR, ODD HAIR, A LIMP, ETC.)?

ANYTHING ELSE UNUSUAL ABOUT THIS CHARACTER'S APPEARANCE?

DESCRIBE YOUR CHARACTER'S MANNERISMS

(HOW DO THEY TALK, WALK, MOVE)

CHARACTER QUESTIONNAIRE

PERSONALITY

DESCRIBE YOUR CHARACTER'S PERSONALITY (LOUD, CHEERFUL, SHY, GRUMPY, ETC.)

DO THEY LIKE TO BE WITH OTHERS, OR DO THEY PREFER TO BE ALONE?

DO THEY HAVE ANY UNUSUAL THINGS ABOUT THE WAY THEY ACT?

CHARACTER'S PAST

DID THEY HAVE A GOOD UPBRINGING OR NOT?

DID ANYTHING BAD HAPPEN TO YOUR CHARACTER THAT FORMED WHO THEY ARE TODAY?

WHERE ARE THEY FROM?

WHO IS YOUR CHARACTER CLOSEST TO? (THIS CAN BE WITHIN THE STORY OR INCLUDE OTHERS NOT IN THE STORY AS WELL)

EMOTIONS

WHO WOULD THEY TALK TO IF THEY NEED A FRIEND??

DO THEY CONNECT WITH OTHERS EASILY, OR DO THEY HAVE TROUBLE MAKING FRIENDS?

THEIR PART IN THE STORY

DO THEY HAVE A MINOR ROLE OR A SIGNIFICANT ROLE IN THE STORY?

DO THE EVENTS OF THE STORY CHANGE THIS CHARACTER, OR DO THEY STAY MOSTLY THE SAME?

WHAT DOES YOUR CHARACTER WANT MOST IN THE STORY? BE AS SPECIFIC AS POSSIBLE

IS THIS CHARACTER A GOOD OR A BAD CHARACTER?

IF AN ANTAGONIST, WHY ARE THEY BAD/EVIL?

HOW DOES YOUR CHARACTER GO AFTER WHAT THEY WANT?

IF THEY DON'T GO AFTER IT, WHY NOT?

CHARACTER TRAITS

Every character has good and bad personality traits, and as the author, you'll have to determine what kind of personality each of your characters have. Below is a list of just some traits you might attribute to your characters—you can use it as a starting block as you develop your novel.

ACTIONS SPEAK LOUDER THAN WORDS

When you choose a word to describe a character, imagine what they've done to deserve that description. If you call them impulsive, imagine a past action they've done that was impulsive. If you call them argumentative, imagine an incident they had with someone where they wouldn't stop arguing.

- ☐ Adventurous
- ☐ Aloof
- ☐ Antisocial
- ☐ Argumentative
- ☐ Arrogant
- ☐ Boisterous
- ☐ Bold
- ☐ Bossy
- ☐ Brave
- ☐ Capable
- ☐ Careful
- ☐ Charming
- ☐ Cheerful
- ☐ Compassionate
- ☐ Competent
- ☐ Conceited
- ☐ Confident
- ☐ Conscientious
- ☐ Considerate
- ☐ Cooperative
- ☐ Courageous
- ☐ Cowardly
- ☐ Creative
- ☐ Cruel
- ☐ Daring
- ☐ Deceptive
- ☐ Decisive
- ☐ Dependable
- ☐ Determined
- ☐ Dishonest
- ☐ Disloyal
- ☐ Disrespectful
- ☐ Dominant
- ☐ Encouraging
- ☐ Enthusiastic
- ☐ Exuberant
- ☐ Fair
- ☐ Fearless
- ☐ Fidgety
- ☐ Finicky
- ☐ Friendly
- ☐ Funny
- ☐ Greedy
- ☐ Grumpy
- ☐ Happy
- ☐ Heartless
- ☐ Helpful
- ☐ Homebody
- ☐ Honest
- ☐ Humble
- ☐ Imaginative
- ☐ Impulsive
- ☐ Independent
- ☐ Indifferent
- ☐ Insensitive
- ☐ Introverted
- ☐ Kind
- ☐ Laid-back
- ☐ Lazy
- ☐ Loyal
- ☐ Mean
- ☐ Meticulous
- ☐ Obnoxious
- ☐ Optimistic
- ☐ Outgoing
- ☐ Patient
- ☐ Persistent
- ☐ Persuasive
- ☐ Pessimistic
- ☐ Picky
- ☐ Pompous
- ☐ Quick-to-Anger
- ☐ Reckless
- ☐ Reliable
- ☐ Resourceful
- ☐ Responsible
- ☐ Romantic
- ☐ Rowdy
- ☐ Rude
- ☐ Self-assured
- ☐ Selfish
- ☐ Shy
- ☐ Silly
- ☐ Smart
- ☐ Sneaky
- ☐ Sociable
- ☐ Solitary
- ☐ Stingy
- ☐ Stubborn
- ☐ Sullen
- ☐ Surly
- ☐ Sympathetic
- ☐ Talkative
- ☐ Thoughtless
- ☐ Timid
- ☐ Trustworthy
- ☐ Understanding
- ☐ Unreliable
- ☐ Unsympathetic
- ☐ Upbeat

CHOOSE THE POINT OF VIEW

The Point of View is all about who's telling your story and how it's told to your readers.

Write a paragraph from your story from the three different perspectives (don't worry—it can be a rough draft!). This will make it easier to choose which point of view will be right for your novel.

FIRST PERSON?
Do I want my main character to tell the story?

THIRD PERSON?
Do I want to tell the story ABOUT my main character?

OMNISCIENT?
Do I want to show what all the characters are thinking?

POINT OF VIEW

FIRST PERSON

The character is inside the story, talking directly to the reader.

THIRD PERSON

An outside narrator follows one character around and describes his/her/their thoughts and actions.

OMNISCIENT

An outside narrator relates the story through the thoughts and actions of all the characters. Beware!

DECIDE ON LOCATIONS AND SETTING

The location, or as we say in writing, the setting, is the place or world where everything happens. If your story is an adventure story, the setting might be a jungle in South America or a desert in Egypt. If your story is science fiction, it might be the planet XR-10. You get the picture.

SETTING

WHAT MOOD OR ATMOSPHERE DO YOU WANT THE STORY TO HAVE? DARK AND CREEPY? BRIGHT AND SUNNY?

IS THE SETTING REAL OR FICTIONAL? DO YOU WANT TO RESEARCH SOMEWHERE YOU'VE NEVER BEEN, OR WRITE ABOUT SOMEPLACE YOU KNOW?

IS IT A SMALL OR LARGE SCALE LOCATION? SMALL TOWN? BIG CITY? INSIDE A BASEBOARD? OUTER SPACE?

DO YOUR CHARACTERS KNOW THIS PLACE OR IS IT NEW TO THEM?

WHAT YEAR IS IT?

WHAT TIME OF YEAR IS IT?

WHERE DOES YOUR MAIN CHARACTER LIVE? WHO LIVES WITH THEM?

STEP 6

PLAN YOUR STORY'S PLOT

Now that you have a good idea of how plot points and story elements work in a novel, you are ready to plot out your book! Take your one-page story version of your book and try your hand at filling out the worksheet on the following pages. You might want to use a pencil so you can make changes as you go.

As you fill it out, remember it doesn't have to be just right from the get-go. Play around with different ideas! This is brainstorming time. The possibilities are endless.

Have fun and see what you come up with!

PLOT NOTES

ACT 1

THE BEGINNING

MAJOR PLOT POINTS

OPENING

The opening introduces the protagonist or main character, gives the readers a feel for what kind of story it will be, and offers a "hook."

SETUP

This section introduces the world, other important characters (such as friends or enemies), and hints at the conflict.

INCITING INCIDENT

This event launches the main events of the story. It comes as a surprise to the protagonist and could be a new problem or opportunity.

CALL TO ACTION

After the Inciting Incident, the protagonist must react to the new reality. What will the character do as a result of the Inciting Incident?

ACT 2

THE MIDDLE

PART 1

This is where you throw everything you've got at your characters. Make them suffer!

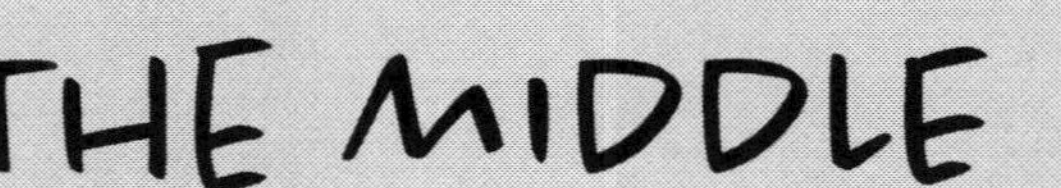

MAJOR PLOT POINTS

THE CHOICE

The protagonist makes active choices as they move forward, trying to reach their story goal.

TRY/FAIL

The protagonist and friends/sidekicks try to solve their problems. They fail a lot, but have some successes as they move toward the story goal.

MIDPOINT/ REVERSAL

Some unexpected revelation sends the story in a new direction, and the stakes are raised. The protagonist may doubt if they can really do this.

ACT 2

PART 2

RIGHT AFTER THE MIDDLE

You've thrown so many obstacles and challenges at your hero, they don't know if they can go on.

ATTACK & BAD GUYS REGROUP

The protagonist tries to keep going in try/fails, but the bad guys now see a serious threat and ramp up their attacks.

MAJOR PLOT POINTS

DARK MOMENT

Things are the worst they've ever been. The protagonist loses hope and nearly gives up. There seems to be no way forward.

TURNING POINT

Something offers hope (a new idea, lucky break, an unseen friend comes through). The protagonist decides to keep going.

ACT 3

END

With the climax and the resolution, the third act leaves the protagonist and other characters with a new understanding of who they really are.

MAJOR PLOT POINTS

A NEW PLAN

The protagonist forms a new plan to reach the story goal, energized by the new info or energy from the Turning Point.

CLIMAX

This is the biggest moment of the whole story. It's what the action has been building toward. The protagonist and team give their all to reach their goal and defeat any antagonists.

RESOLUTION

After the Climax, this is a period of resolving unfinished parts to your story and showing the protagonist living life in the new world after the antagonist has been defeated.

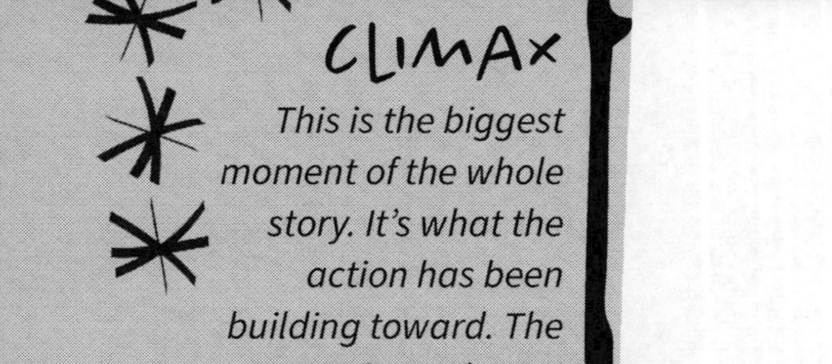

STEP 7

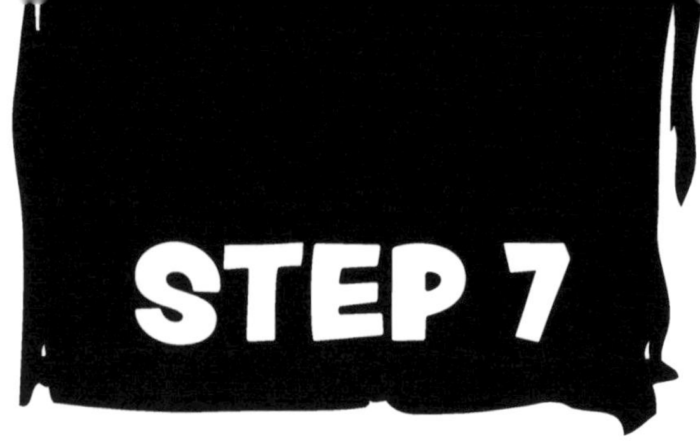

DIVIDE THE PLOT INTO CHAPTERS

As you plot out your novel and put the events in order, you'll break up the story into different Chapters.

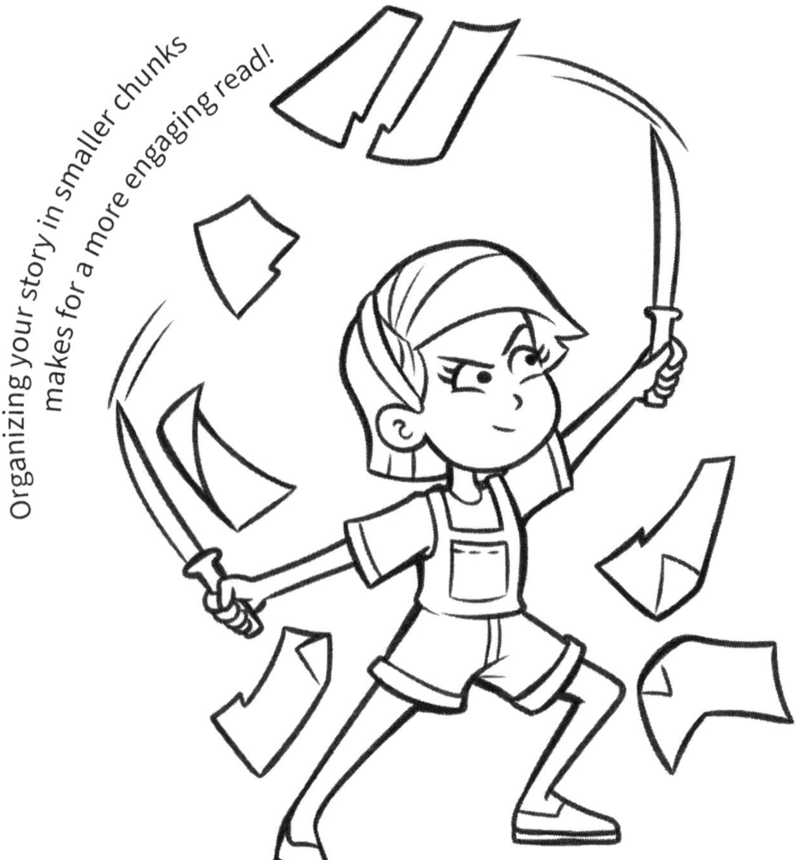
Organizing your story in smaller chunks
makes for a more engaging read!

ACT 1

THE BEGINNING

CHAPTER BREAKS

OPENING
Try for 2 chapters
Introduce the protagonist and give the readers a feel for the story.

SETUP
Try for 2 chapters
Introduce the world (setting) and hint at the conflict.

INCITING INCIDENT
Try for 3 chapters
Launch the main events of the story; introduce the conflict/problem.

CALL TO ACTION
Try for 3 chapters
Reaction to the new reality. What will the character do as a result of the Inciting Incident?

DON'T FORGET ABOUT THE HOOK

ACT 1 SHOULD BE 25% OF YOUR BOOK

THAT'S ABOUT **10 CHAPTERS** OF A 40,000 WORD BOOK

ACT 2

PART 1
THE MIDDLE

The protagonist starts to take action.

THE CHOICE

Try for 3 chapters

The protagonist tries to solve the problem with some success and some failures.

TRY/FAIL

Try for 3 chapters

Unexpected revelations change the story; the protagonist has doubts.

MIDPOINT/REVERSAL

Try for 4 chapters

PART 2 CHAPTER BREAKS
RIGHT **AFTER** THE MIDDLE

The bad guys/conflict get even worse
ATTACK & BAD BUYS REGROUP
Try for 3 chapters

Things are as bad as they can possibly get. The protagonist loses all hope.
DARK MOMENT
Try for 3 chapters

Something offers hope and the protagonist keeps going.
TURNING POINT
Try for 4 chapters

ACT 2 SHOULD BE 50% OF YOUR BOOK
THAT'S ABOUT 20 CHAPTERS OF A 40,000 WORD BOOK

ACT 3

END
CHAPTER BREAKS

Energized by a new hope, the protagonist forms a new plan

A NEW PLAN

Try for 3 or 4 chapters

The big moment! Everything has been building up to this and the protagonist either succeeds or fails.

CLIMAX

Try for 4 or 5 chapters

Resolve any unfinished business and get used to the new normal.

RESOLUTION

Try for 2 chapters

ACT 3 SHOULD BE 25% OF YOUR BOOK

THAT'S ABOUT **10 CHAPTERS** OF A 40,000 WORD BOOK

CHAPTER NOTES

SET UP SOME ACTION

Your story won't go anywhere if there's no action in it. Think about *what* events you'll write about that will move the story forward. And then think about *how* you'll write those passages so that the reader *feels* like the story is moving forward.

ACTION TIPS

LIST DIFFERENT EVENTS AND INCIDENTS—BIG OR SMALL—THAT YOU'RE GOING TO INCLUDE IN YOUR NOVEL THAT WILL ADD ACTION TO YOUR STORY.

Use strong action verbs

Have characters interact with one another—dialogue moves faster than description

Describe character movements during dialogue

Use shorter sentences to increase the pace

Include events that make the plot move forward (this happened, so this other thing happened...)

Make sure your subplots add to the story

Keep your descriptive passages relevant and not too long

Add cliffhangers—put your characters in jeopardy

WRITE GREAT DIALOGUE

Write a short conversation between two of your characters where one is daring the other to eat a chocolate-covered grasshopper.

WHAT PERSUASIVE ARGUMENTS WILL THEY USE?

HOW WILL THE OTHER KID—OR ADULT!—TRY TO TALK THEIR WAY OUT OF IT?

ARE THEY SPEAKING SLOWLY OR QUICKLY?

WHAT KIND OF ACTIONS ARE HAPPENING AS THEY TALK?

IS THE COAXER LEANING FORWARD, POINTING AT THE GRASSHOPPER? ARE THEY GRINNING? SMIRKING? LAUGHING? ARE THEY PUSHING THE PLATE CLOSER TO THE OTHER CHARACTER?

IS THE COAXEE LEANING BACK, AWAY FROM THE GRASSHOPPER? ARE THEY GRIMACING? TRYING NOT TO GAG?

BUILD THE CLIMAX

This is it! This is what you've been working towards. All the events in your novel culminate in the climax and you're going to make it memorable!

What happens during your climax? List 10 (or more) events or conversations that occur. They can include character actions or reactions, and even thoughts or memories you want them to have. Don't worry if they're not in order—you'll fix that up once you start writing.

REMEMBER

The climax can span a few chapters.

1.
2.
3.
4.
5.
6.
7.
8.
9.
10.
11.
12.
13.
14.
15.
16.
17.
18.
19.
20.
21.
22.

RESOLVE YOUR STORY

After the climax, you need to give your characters (and your readers!) some time to decompress before ending your novel. This is the time to wrap up all the subplots and let your characters get used to the 'new normal.'

Have you tied up all the loose ends? Have you left the reader satisfied? List all your subplots and how you'll end them.

How are you leaving things with your characters? What are their plans now that they've overcome the conflict?

EDIT YOUR DRAFT

Take a good story and make it great!

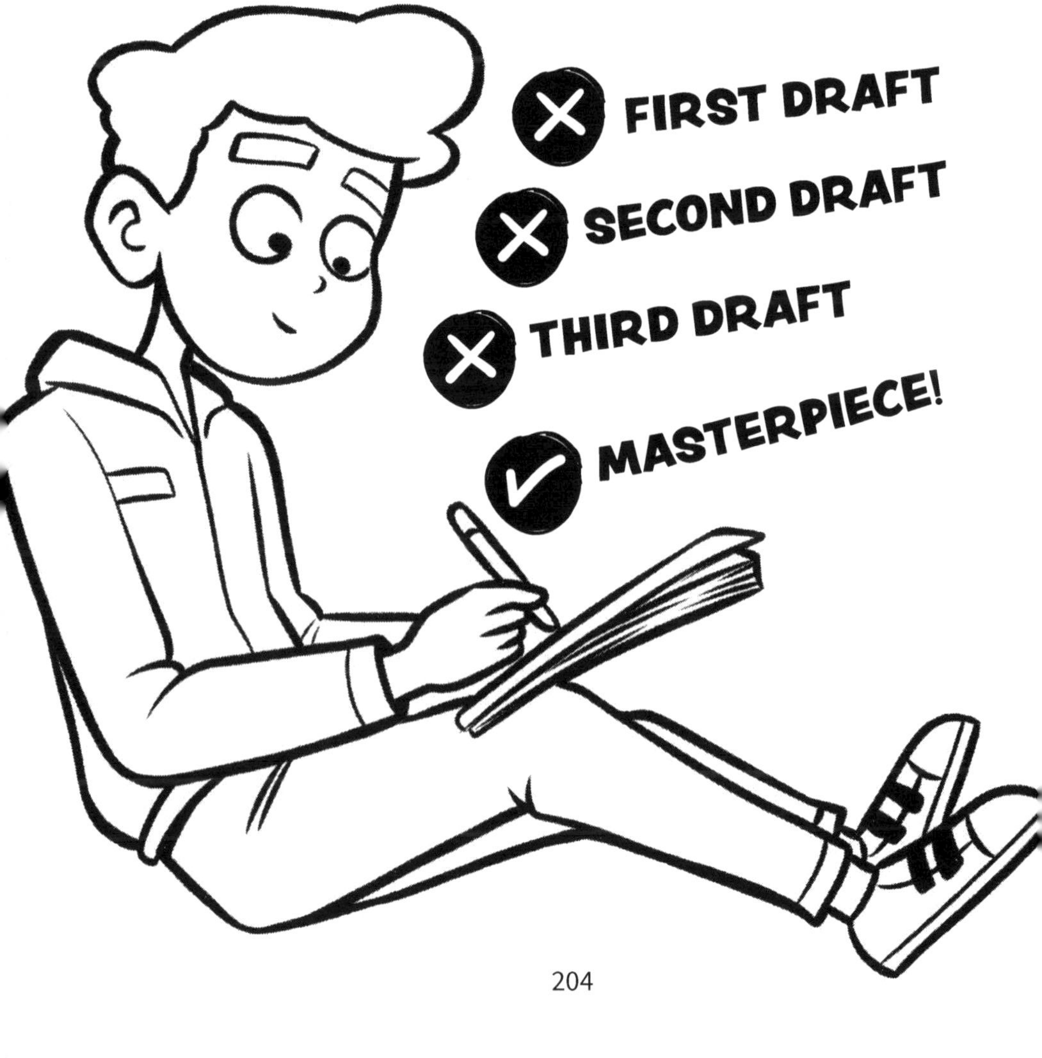

FIRST DRAFT

SECOND DRAFT

THIRD DRAFT

MASTERPIECE!

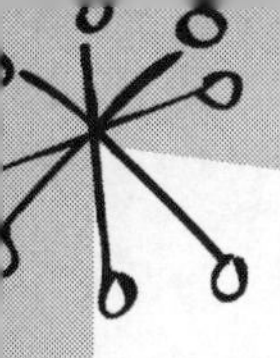

1 STRUCTURAL EDITING

Leave your book aside for at least a week before doing this step. You'll view it more objectively when you come back to it.

Look at the overall story and see if it should be organized differently for a better flow. This is where you would delete sentences or paragraphs, and move passages around.

Focus on the big picture of your story and figure out the best way for it to flow.

2 COPY EDITING

At this stage you go through your text and make sure it's readable and free of grammar mistakes.

Make sure there is no head hopping with your point of view, and no floating heads with your dialogue passages.

Check that all dialogue follows the formatting rules. If you use dialogue tags other than "said," make sure they don't stand out, (generally "said" is best).

Read your book line and by line and make any text changes you see fit.

3 PROOFING

This is the final check—the last stage before it goes to print!

Look for any errors that were missed in the previous passes. This might include double words (the the), missing words, or any inconsistencies.

REMEMBER

It helps to have other people read your novel at all three stages. They'll see things you don't.

FOR A METICULOUS MANUSCRIPT, DO EACH OF THESE STEPS MORE THAN ONCE BEFORE MOVING ON TO THE NEXT ONE

STEP 13

PUBLISH YOUR BOOK

Turn your manuscript into a real book by either going the traditional route, or self-publishing.

TRADITIONAL PUBLISHING

PROS

They take care of the following:

- editing
- formatting
- editing
- design
- illustration
- book launch
- marketing
- sell in stores & online

CONS

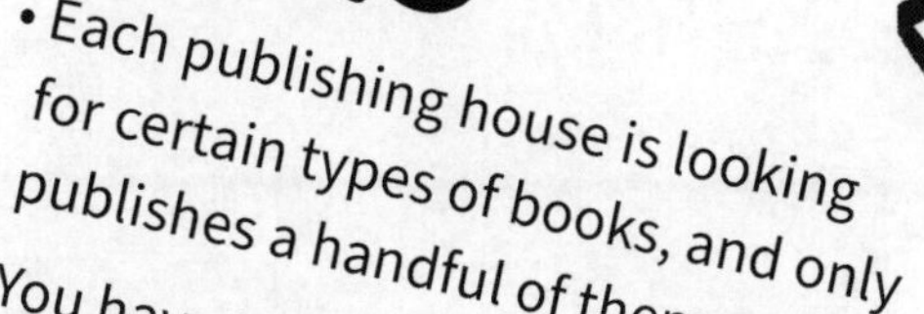

- Each publishing house is looking for certain types of books, and only publishes a handful of them a year.
- You have to find the right publishing house for your type of book by sending numerous query letters.
- If your book is chosen, it could take a year or longer for it to be published.

REMEMBER! AGENTS AND PUBLISHERS WILL NEVER ASK FOR A "READING FEE."

SELF-PUBLISHING

PROS

- You have total control over your book and can publish any book any time you want.
- Upload it to Amazon Kindle Direct Publishing and reach millions of readers.

CONS

You have to take care of the following:

- editing
- formatting
- editing
- design
- illustration
- book launch
- marketing

- If you can't do all of the above yourself, you'll have to hire someone to help.
- The book is only sold online.
- If you don't market it well, no one but your friends and family will see it.

TO BECOMING A PUBLISHED AUTHOR BEFORE YOU TURN 13!

By following the 13 steps and filling out the worksheets, you should have all the information you need to start writing (if you haven't started already!). You might get discouraged at times (you haven't chosen an easy task!), but you can do it!

If you found this book helpful,
I would be incredibly grateful if you took a few moments to leave a review on Amazon.
Thank you!

Ollie Ood

CONCLUSION

Throughout the course of this book, you have learned the necessary steps to take a brand-new baby story idea and turn it into a fully fleshed-out novel. Congratulations! Whether you have worked on your story as you read along or you're just taking your first step now, you are now equipped to write your story and see where it takes you. The possibilities are endless.

Chapter One taught us where stories come from—that mystical place deep within your imagination that draws from all you think, feel, and experience. Story ideas are everywhere if we have the eyes to see them. Slowing down, listening, and encouraging your imagination to come alive is the key to getting in touch with your story idea place.

Chapter Two taught us to take our story idea, a one-or two-line thought, and turn it into a one-page story foundation. This is where we learned to ask story questions such as "What happens when?" We build the rest of a house on the foundation. This one-page story is the foundation for your novel. Just like a well-built home has specific qualifications (a bathroom, a roof, windows, doors), a well-written story has key parts as well. We learned these are Characters, Setting, Plot, Conflict, and Resolution.

Next up, **Chapter Three** explored characters. Why did we look at characters first and not plot? While we certainly could start with the plot, and many others do, it is my opinion that letting your plot and story grow out of the characters creates a richer story. Why? Because the heart of any story has to do with whose story it is and what it means to them. If we create a cool plot and plug any old characters into it, it may be a fun ride, but it won't have the depth of a character-driven story. But there are many thoughts on this in the writing world, and you must find your own way and become your own storyteller.

We also learned how to fill out a Character Questionnaire, how to narrow in on what your character wants, and how to create captivating villains.

For **Chapter Four**, we learned about Point of View (POV). Hopefully, diving into all the potential ways to tell your story made you feel excited at all the opportunities and not overwhelmed! As a refresher, here are the three most common points of view used in fiction today:

1 - ***First Person*** – A character, usually the main character, tells us the story.

2 - ***Third Person*** – An outside narrator, not a character, tells us the story and is limited to what one character can see.

3 - ***Omniscient*** – An outside narrator, not a character, tells us the story and is not limited to one character. They can see and know everything.

Chapter Five explored setting. We learned about the dangers of too little description (characters floating against a blank background) and too much description (the story slowed down by way too much information). As you move forward with your novel, keep in mind the formula:

Setting = a few carefully chosen details + noticed by my character + when they are feeling X.

Your descriptions of your setting should not be disconnected from your character and their experiences of the world they find themselves in.

Chapter Six was all about plot. We focused on the qualities of a good story, such as starting in the right place and ending at the right time, and we gave an in-depth look at the Three Act Structure that appears in many stories. Perhaps most importantly, you learned how to plot out a story and learned the important scenes and plot points that should occur in a story and where they take place.

In **Chapter Seven**, you plotted out your novel and learned how to divide your story into chapters and scenes. We also introduced the idea of subplots and discussed how to use them to develop your story further. Often subplots are hiding just below the surface. Is there another story hiding beneath the main one? What about your side characters? What do they want, and why are they going along on the story journey? These are all excellent questions to ask as you look for ways to flesh out your story.

Chapter Eight exploded onto the page as we took a look at Action and Pacing. You learned some of the main culprits for slow pacing—too much backstory, too many subplots, too much time in your character's head. On the flip side, we discussed tips to help the active sections of your book have a faster pace, such as using shorter scenes, more dialogue, and inserting time bombs and cliffhangers.

In **Chapter Nine**, we learned the proper way to format dialogue and create dialogue that sounds natural, isn't cluttered up with too many filler words such as "like" and "um," and that is consistent with the character. What does "consistent to the character" mean? If you are writing for your grandma, you wouldn't have her say, "What up, dude!" Unless, of course, your grandma talks like that.

Chapter Ten discussed one of the most critical parts of your whole book, the climax. Remember that "the climax is the moment in the story that everything has been moving toward. It will decide the fate of everything." We explored ways to ramp up the intensity as your book grows close to the climax, such as increasing the internal and external conflicts and using your setting and scene length to add to the energy.

In **Chapter Eleven**, we slowed things down and looked at the role of resolution in storytelling. After all, you can't just end everything the moment someone gets saved from hanging off the skyscraper, right? Resolving the loose ends, letting your readers slow back down to everyday life, and leaving them with a great final feeling for the end of the book are all parts of an excellent resolution.

Chapter Twelve explored what to do after you write "The End." We learned to fight the urge to publish right away or share your story with everyone you know. Remember, every novel goes through many drafts, and yours should take what is good and make it better, and then take what is better and make it great.

Lastly, in **Chapter Thirteen**, we learned about the two paths to publishing: Traditional and Self-publication. There are pros and cons to each approach, but I hope you found some guidance as you navigate the final step in creating your novel.

My hope in writing this book is that you are inspired to write one of your own. Whether you publish your novel or not, you should feel proud of the fantastic accomplishment of writing and completing your first novel.

And if you haven't written it yet, what are you waiting for? Get started today! I hope one day you can hold the book in your hands that you worked so hard on.

References

Chapter Two

Barber, Michael. (1977, September 25). John Le Carré: An Interrogation. Retrieved from https://archive.nytimes.com/www.nytimes.com/books/99/03/21/specials/lecarre-interrogation.html

Chapter Three

Hay, Lucy V. (2021, May 6). How to Create a Detailed Character Profile. Retrieved from https://www.wikihow.com/Create-a-Detailed-Character-Profile

Chapter Eight

Pacing in Writing: 10 Powerful Ways to Keep Readers Hooked. (2018, October 13). Retrieved from https://blog.reedsy.com/pacing-in-writing/

Chapter Ten

Jordan. (2017, November 23). Story Climax Examples: Writing Gripping Build-ups. Retrieved from https://www.nownovel.com/blog/story-climax-examples-tips/

Chapter Eleven

Weiland. K.M. (2012, May 6). The Secrets of Story Structure, Pt. 11: The Resolution.

Retrieved from https://www.helpingwritersbecomeauthors.com/secrets-of-story-structure-pt-11/

Chapter Thirteen

Jenkins, Jerry. (2021). How to Publish a Book: My Ultimate Guide From 40+ Years of Experience. Retrieved from https://jerryjenkins.com/how-to-publish-a-book/

Conclusion

Nash, Jenny. (2018, January 9). Be So Good They Can't Ignore You. Retrieved from https://medium.com/no-blank-pages/be-so-good-they-cant-ignore-you-6da4ff35bfe9

Youth Author Biographies

Greven, Alec

Alec Greven. (2019, October 5). Retrieved from https://en.wikipedia.org/wiki/Alec_Greven

Guptara, Saresh and Jyoti

Biography: Saresh and Jyoti. (n.d.). Retrieved from https://twins.guptara.net/?page_id=3

Hinton, S.E.

Biography. (n.d.). Retrieved from http://www.sehinton.com/bio.html

Graham, Ginnie. (2017, May 5). Forever an Outsider: Tulsa author S.E. Hinton looks back 50 years to her first book. Retrieved from https://tulsaworld.com/lifestyles/magazine/forever-an-outsider-author-s-e-hinton-looks-back-50-years-to-her-first/article_ce9a7027-c470-50f3-82f0-3a993cd2f768.html

Korman, Gordan

Korman, Gordan. (n.d.). About Gordan Korman. Retrieved from https://gordonkorman.com/more-resources/about-gordon-korman-2

Marcionette, Jake

Gillis, Michele. (2015, November 4). Published at 12, young author wants to inspire others. Retrieved from https://www.jacksonville.com/article/20151104/NEWS/801256471

Paolini, Christopher

Christopher Paolini. (n.d.). Retrieved from https://www.paolini.net/biographies/christopher-paolini-full/

Index

Acknowledgments

This was such a fun book to work on and I hope it helps kids not only believe that they can write a novel, but helps them take the steps to see it through. I want to thank the people who helped me proof and edit it: Morgan Wyman, Samantha Crothers, Ray Yuen, and Paul Panchyshyn. I especially want to thank Elaine Cox, without whom this book would literally not exist.

Beta Readers

I want to extend a big thank you to my beta readers—they gave me some great input and made some really helpful comments.

Daemon Mouck
Jack Hipolito
Jane Hipolito
Georgia Sewell
Luke Sewell
Daniel Wisniewski

CalamariTales.com

Made in the USA
Monee, IL
16 December 2021